国家出版基金项目
NATIONAL PUBLICATION FOUNDATION

CHINESE RED
中国红

武 术

Chinese Martial Arts

蒋剑民 黄一棉 ◎ 编著

全 国 百 佳 图 书 出 版 单 位
APGTIME 时代出版传媒股份有限公司
时代出版 黄 山 书 社

图书在版编目(CIP)数据

武术：汉英对照 /蒋剑民，黄一棉编著. ——合肥：黄山书社, 2012.3
（中国红）
ISBN 978-7-5461-2720-0

Ⅰ. ①武… Ⅱ. ①蒋…②黄… Ⅲ. ①武术—介绍—中国—汉、英 Ⅳ. ①G852

中国版本图书馆CIP数据核字(2012)第033740号

武术
WU SHU

蒋剑民，黄一棉 编著

出 版 人：任耕耘
责任编辑：司 雯   特约编辑：朱昌爱
责任印制：戚 帅 李 磊   装帧设计：商子庄

出版发行：时代出版传媒股份有限公司（http://www.press-mart.com）
　　　　　黄山书社（http://www.hsbook.cn）
　　　　　（合肥市蜀山区翡翠路1118号出版传媒广场7层　邮编：230071）
经　　销：新华书店   营销电话：0551-3533762　3533768
印　　刷：合肥精艺印刷有限公司   电　　话：0551-4859368

开　本：710×875　1/16   印张：12   字数：155千字
版　次：2012年6月第1版　　2012年6月第1次印刷
书　号：ISBN 978-7-5461-2720-0   定价：59.00元

中国武术又称"国术"，是中国传统的体育项目。武术是由远古时期人类的搏击与格斗方法演变而来，以踢、打、摔、拿等攻防格斗的动作为基础，按照一定规律编排成各种攻防格斗套路，在技击格斗的同时，又具有强身健体、培养意志的作用。

中国武术有着悠久的历史和博大精深的文化体系，是中华文明中的瑰宝和中华民族智慧的结晶。在漫长的发展过程中，武术广集技击精华，以传统哲学和伦理学为思想基础，以传统兵家学说和中医学为科学依据，内修

Chinese Martial Arts (*Wushu*), also known as "art of the nation", is a traditional Chinese sports event. Evolved from the ways of human fighting and combat in ancient times, martial arts utilizes offensive and defensive combat actions such as kicks, punches, wrestling and takedowns as its foundation, and arranges them into a variety of offensive and defensive combat routines according to certain rules. Aside from its application in fighting and combat, martial arts also functions to build up physical fitness and develop will power.

Chinese Martial Arts boasts a long history and an extensive and profound cultural system. It is a treasure of Chinese civilization as well as the crystallization of Chinese people's wisdom. In its long process

外练，术道并重，开创了较为系统的技击体系和众多门派的中国功夫，形成了独具民族风貌的武术文化体系。

本书着重介绍了中国武术的源流、门派、拳术、十八般武艺，以及武术的思想文化内涵，帮助读者从武术中窥见中华文化，进一步了解中国传统文化的精神实质。

of development, martial arts has gathered a wide variety of combat essence, established its ideological foundation on traditional philosophy and ethics, and based its scientific root upon the doctrines of traditional military strategists and traditional Chinese medicine to perform internal cultivation and external trainings with equal importance attached to the techniques as well as the principles. Martial arts have created well-organized martial arts systems and numerous sects of Chinese kung fu (another alias for Chinese Martial Arts), and has formed a cultural system of martial arts with unique national features.

This book highlights the origins, sects, fist fighting techniques and versatile techniques of Chinese Martial Arts, as well as the ideological and cultural connotations in martial arts to help readers get a glimpse of Chinese culture in the light of martial arts, and to obtain a better understanding of the spiritual essence of traditional Chinese culture.

目 录 Contents

十八般兵器
Eighteen Weapons of Chinese Martial Arts ... 147

武术的起源、发展
Origin and Development of Martial Arts

　　中国武术文化源远流长，萌芽于原始社会(起自大约170万年前的元谋猿人，止于公元前21世纪夏王朝的建立)人类对自然、社会环境进行抗争的过程，随着军事战争的发展，从简单的搏击，逐渐成熟完备，自成体系，出现了各种徒手和器械套路。

The long history of the Chinese Martial Arts culture started from the primitive society (starting from Homo erectus Yuanmouensis around 1.7 million years ago and ending in the establishment of the Xia Dynasty in the 21st century B.C.). In the process of their struggle against nature and the social environment, people came up with simple moves of fighting, which gradually matured along with the development of militaristic wars and developed into various systems of barehanded and weapon-tool routines.

> 武术的缘起

武术是一门综合性的运动，以格斗技能为基础，其招式都是按照攻防的格斗要求设计出来的，并结合了狩猎、战争、武舞等元素逐渐发展形成。

武术的起源可以追溯至原始社会，其萌生与发展与人类的生存竞争和原始战争分不开。在早期的人类社会中，格斗的对象不是人，而

• 石球(旧石器时代)
Stone Ball (the Paleolithic Period)

> Origin of Martial Arts

Martial Arts is comprehensive exercise based upon fighting skills. It has its movements designed in accordance with the requirements in offensive and defensive fighting and incorporates combined elements such as hunting, warfare and martial dance in its eventual development and formation.

The origin of Martial Arts can be traced back to the primitive society. Its origin and development cannot be separated from human's survival competition and primitive wars. In the early human society, the opponents in fights were not human beings, but beasts. At that time, living conditions for humans were extremely poor. They lived the life of a savage and burrowed

● 原始人类狩猎图
Hunting Scenes of Primitive People

是野兽。当时人类生存条件非常恶劣，茹毛饮血，穴居野处，到处都是凶禽猛兽。为了生存繁衍，人类不得不与野兽进行殊死搏斗。在中国西部地区的古老岩画中就有许多描绘人与野兽搏斗的场面。在狩猎的过程中，人们逐渐形成了奔跑、跳跃、滚翻、躲闪、拳打、脚踢等徒手的技击动作，以及运用石制、木制棍棒等工具的技能，积累一些攻防经验。

原始工具的出现与进化，也是原始技击产生与发展的有力证

in the wild, where beasts and predators were everywhere. In order to survive and procreate, mankind had no choice but to engage in death struggles against beasts. Many ancient rock paintings in the western region of China depicted various scenes of struggle between men and beasts. In the process of hunting, people gradually formulated unarmed fighting techniques, such as running, jumping, rolling, dodging, punching, kicking and the like, as well as skills to utilize stone and wooden tools like clubs. A number of offensive and defensive experiences were thus accumulated.

明。旧石器时代（约250万年—约1万年）出现了粗糙的用石头打制的尖状器、砍砸器，到新石器时代（八九千年前）出现了磨制精细的木质、石质、骨制工具，特别是弓箭的发明，大大提高了人们打猎的能力，扩大了狩猎的范围。

The emergence and evolution of primitive tools were also powerful proof of the emergence and development of primitive forms of fighting techniques. Sharp-pointed wares and chopping tools roughly wrought from stones emerged during the Paleolithic Period (around 2.5 million to 10,000 years ago). During the Neolithic Age (approx. 8500-4500 years ago), well-wrought tools made of fine wood, stones and bones came into being, and the invention of bows and arrows, in particular, greatly enhanced human's ability to hunt, and expanded the scope of the hunting range.

● 骨镞(新石器时代)
骨镞是骨制的箭头，是一种常用的狩猎工具。
Bone Arrowhead (the Neolithic Age)
The arrowhead was made out of bone. It was a very common hunting tool.

● 内蒙古鄂温克族狩猎岩画
岩画表现了一群手持弓箭的猎人围猎一头驼鹿的场面，具有浓厚的原始集体狩猎时代的气息。
Rock Paintings of Hunting of the Ewenke Tribe in Inner Mongolia
The rock painting depicted the scene of a group of hunters armed with bows and arrows hunting for a moose, which delivered a strong atmosphere in the era of primitive collective hunting.

除了狩猎以外，原始时期的战争与武术的萌芽也关系紧密。原始社会中，各个部落为了争夺食物、领地，或为争夺首领的地位，常常发生争斗。这些人与人之间的争斗，促进了原始武术的形成。到了原始社会末期，以掠夺奴隶和财富为目的的部落战争越来越频繁，规模也越来越大。中国古代传说中黄帝轩辕氏与蚩尤九黎部落之间的战争，就运用了比较先进的青铜兵器，人们的格斗技术也比狩猎要复杂得多，这种原始战争促进了武术的发展。

In addition to hunting, the beginning of martial arts was also closely related to primitive wars. In the primitive society, tribes often battled against each other in order to compete for food, territory or the position of leadership. These struggles among human beings promoted the formation of primitive martial arts. Towards the end of the primitive society, tribal warfare for the purpose of plundering slaves and wealth became more and more frequent, and the scale grew larger and larger. In ancient China, legend had it that advanced bronze weapons were utilized during the war

• 黄帝战蚩尤
Battle between the Yellow Emperor and Chiyou

原始武术的发展与原始教育、原始宗教，以及原始娱乐是分不开的。在原始教育中，传授与训练生产经验、战斗技术是一项重要的内容。原始人类在祭祀求神、娱乐等活动中，模拟狩猎或战争的场景，执各种兵器手舞足蹈，以巧妙的动作展现自己的敏捷拳脚。这种原始的舞蹈与武艺的演练是分不开的。在古籍《尚书·尧典》中记载，一个名叫"夔"的首领说："於！予击石拊石，百兽率舞。"（啊！让我们敲打起石鼓，和百兽一起跳起来吧！）这里的"百兽"，指的是模拟野兽的形态动作，是一种狩猎舞，也是古代武术中象形拳最原始的萌芽。

• 左江岩画中的武舞图 (图片提供：FOTOE)
Martial Dance Illustrated in the Zuojiang Rock Paintings

between Yellow Emperor Xuanyuan and Chiyou of the Jiuli tribe, and the fighting techniques used by the people were also more complex than those in hunting. Such primitive wars had promoted the development of martial arts.

The development of primitive martial arts is also inseparable from primitive education, primitive religion as well as primitive entertainment. The teaching and training of both production experiences and fighting techniques are important contents of primitive education. In the worshipping and entertaining activities among others, primitive people used to simulate hunting or war scenes, dancing around with various weapons held in their hands to demonstrate their agile fighting skills with delicate movements. In the classic *Yao Dian* (Document about Yao) of *The Book of History*, it was recorded that a leader called Kui said: "Ah, let us hit the stone drums, so all the beasts can dance together!" The "beasts" mentioned here indicates a form of movement in imitation of animals. It was a form of hunting dance and the most primitive form of the ancient animal-style martial arts.

In the primitive society, hunting, tribal conflicts and primitive dances all

原始社会中的狩猎、部落间的争斗和原始舞蹈对武术的产生，起着直接的促进作用。但武术毕竟不同于狩猎、打仗和舞蹈，它的形成和发展还需要更加充分的条件，中国悠久的历史给了中华民族发展武术的时间和条件。

exercised direct effects in promoting the emergence of martial arts. However, martial arts are different from hunting, warring and dancing. It requires more adequate conditions in order to be formed and developed. China's long history has provided the time and conditions needed for Chinese people to develop Chinese martial arts.

> 武术的发展

　　武术形成于中国奴隶社会时期。启改变了原始社会部落联盟民主推选首领的禅让制度，建立了中国历史上第一个世袭的奴隶制国家夏朝（约前2070—前1600），引起了东夷部落的起兵反抗。东夷人善于使用弓箭，有很多神箭手，神话传说中的射日英雄后羿就曾做过他们的首领。夏朝为了镇压东夷部落的反抗，非常重视军事演练，集中军队进行击刺练习。经过连绵不断的战火，武术为了适应实战的需要，进一步向实用化、规范化发展。

　　商周时期（前1600—前256），频繁激烈的军事斗争，不仅促使武器由简单到复杂，向多样化发展，还促进了攻防格斗技术的提高和发

> Development of Martial Arts

Martial Arts was formed in China during the period of the slave society. Qi changed the throne abdication system used by the tribal alliance to democratically elect a leader in the primitive society, and established the first hereditary state of slave society in China, the Xia Dynasty (approx.2070 B.C.–1600 B.C.), which ignited revolts from the Dongyi tribes. The Dongyi tribes were good at the skills of bows and arrows and had many legendary archers. In the legend of Chinese mythology, Houyi, the hero who shot the redundant suns, was once their leader. In order to suppress the Dongyi resistance, the Xia Dynasty attached great importance to military exercises and focused on the practice of striking attacks in the army. Through an

后羿射日

相传后羿是夏朝东夷族的首领，善于射箭。当时天上有十个太阳，把土地烤焦了，庄稼都枯干了，人们热得喘不过气来，有的倒在地上昏迷不醒。因为天气酷热的缘故，一些怪禽猛兽也都从干涸的江湖和火焰似的森林里跑出来，在各地残害百姓。后羿看到人们生活在苦难中，便决心射掉多余的九个太阳。他带着弓箭，翻山越岭来到东海边。后羿拉弓射箭，把箭一支一支地向炽热的太阳射去。顷刻间十个太阳被射去了九个，只留下一个太阳，让人类万物繁衍生息下去。

Houyi Shoots the Suns

According to the legend, Houyi, leader of the Dongyi tribe in the Xia Dynasty, was good at archery. At that time, there were not one but ten suns roaming the sky, which scorched the land and withered the crops; people were out of breath or fell into comas because of the heat. Due to this extreme heat, strange fowls and beasts also came out of dried lakes and flame-like forests to harm humans everywhere. Seeing people living in misery, Houyi decided to shoot down the nine extra suns. Armed with his bow and arrows, he tramped over hills and dales and arrived at the East Sea coast. Shooting his arrows one by one towards the arrogant suns, Houyi instantly shot down nine of the suns, leaving only one sun in the sky for humans to thrive on.

• 石函上的《后羿射日图》（汉）（图片提供：FOTOE）
图中乌鸦代表太阳。
Picture of *Houyi Shooting the Suns* on the Stone Casket (Han Dynasty, 206 B.C.- 220 A.D.)
In the picture, the crows represented the suns.

纪昌学箭

纪昌学箭的故事出自《列子》，相传战国列御寇著。飞卫是古时候的一位射箭能手，箭无虚发，百发百中。纪昌便拜飞卫为师学习射箭。飞卫收纪昌为徒后，对他说："你要先学会盯住一个目标不眨眼，然后才谈得上学射箭。"纪昌回到家，躺在妻子的织布机下，眼睛盯着妻子织布时踩动的踏脚板，坚持练了两年，即使锥子的尖刺到眼眶，他的双眼也一眨不眨。于是纪昌又去找飞卫，飞卫却说："这样还不够，还要练好眼力。直到你能把细微的东西看得清清楚楚，再回来找我。"纪昌回去后，用牦牛尾巴的毛把虱子挂在窗户上，每天目不转睛地注视着虱子。过了三年，纪昌眼中的虱子变得很清晰，他用箭能射穿虱子的中心。纪昌赶快去告诉飞卫，飞卫高兴地说："你已经把射箭的功夫学到了"。

Ji Chang's Learning of Archery

The story of Ji Chang learning archery came from *Liezi,* a book collecting the works by Liezi, a thinker from the Warring States Period (475 B.C.-221 B.C.), and his disciples. Fei Wei was an archery expert in ancient times. His arrows were never shot in vain and no target was missed by his shot. Ji Chang hoped to learn archery and asked Fei Wei to apprentice him. After accepting Ji Chang as his disciple, Fei Wei told him: "You have to learn to stare at a target and never blink, and then we will talk about learning archery." When Ji Chang returned home, he lay under his wife's loom and stared at the foot pedal as his wife weaved. After two years of practice, even if the tip of the shuttle reached his eye socket, Ji Chang would not blink. Ji Chang then visited Fei Wei again, but Fei Wei said: "This is not enough. Once you've trained your eyes to the point that they can discriminate the minute details clearly, come back to me again." After returning from the visit, Ji Chang hung a yak's tail with lice in the hair by the window, and began to stare at it every day. After three years, the lice became so clear and articulate in Ji Chang's sight that he was able to drive his arrow into the center of a louse. Ji Chang then hurried back to Fei Wei, who happily told him: "You've already learned the arts of archery."

展。战争中主要的作战形式是车战，战车上有善于驾驭的士兵、弓箭手和拿着长矛的击刺手，车兵是战斗的主力。当时，对士兵的武艺

endless series of wars, martial arts was thus developed further into more practical and standardized applications.

During the Shang and Zhou

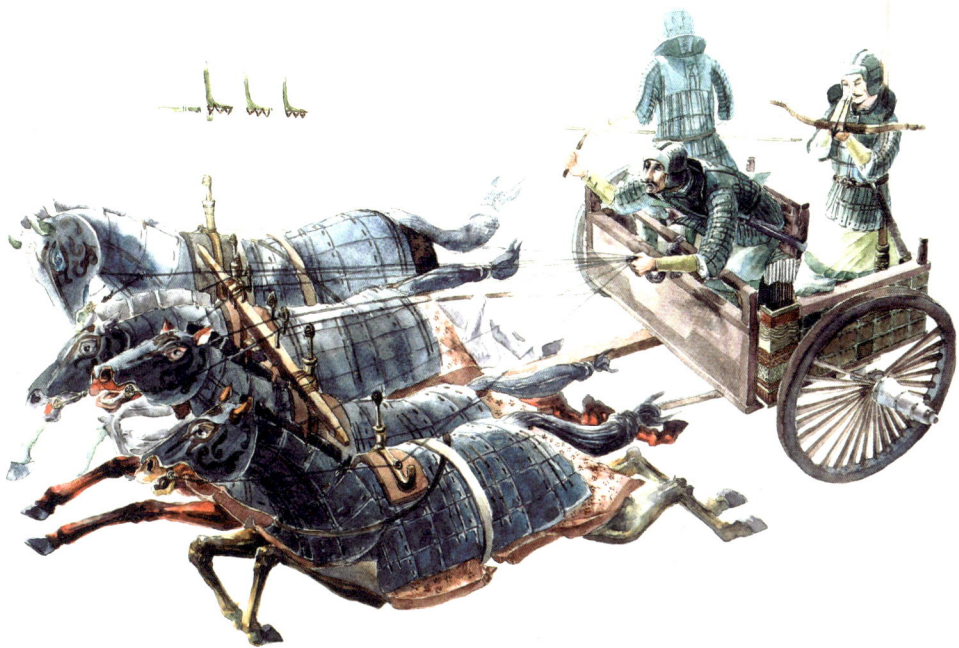

• 商代战车和车兵示意图
Schematic Illustration of Chariots and Chariot
Soldiers in the Shang Dynasty

训练主要体现在体能和简单的兵器使用技术方面。

射箭是商周时期军事武艺训练的重要内容，上至天子诸侯，下至平民百姓，都练习射箭，出现了各种形式的射箭活动。天子举行祭祀、宴会等活动时，有被称做"礼射"的射箭比赛；平民定期举办名为"乡射"的射箭活动。在培养贵

Dynasties (1600 B.C.-256 B.C.), frequent and intense military conflicts not only promoted the development of weapons from simplistic devices to complex and diversified designs, but also facilitated the improvement and development of fighting techniques in offense and defense. The main form of combat in the war was chariot combat, where the chariot carried skillful charioteers, archers and spear

● 长脊窄翼铜镞（商）
A Long-ridge and Narrow-wing Bronze Arrowhead (Shang Dynasty, 1600 B.C.-1046 B.C.)

族子弟的学校里，射箭被列为六艺之一。

商周时期，军队利用武舞（一种使用武器的操练形式）来训练士兵，鼓舞士气。士兵们手拿武器，列队整齐，舞姿粗犷，气势逼人。

春秋战国时期（前770—前

fighters. Chariot soldiers were the main force in battles. At that time, soldiers' martial arts training was mainly reflected in their physical performances and their skills in using simple weapons.

During the Shang and Zhou Dynasties, archery was the major part of military training on martial arts. With emperors and nobles at the top and civilians and peasants at the bottom, archery was practiced almost by everyone. Various types of archery events were held. When rituals, banquets and other activities were hosted by the emperor, an archery event called *Li She* (ritual shot) was held. Civilians, on the other hand, regularly organized an archery event called *Xiang She* (rural shot). In schools that trained children of the nobility, archery was listed as one of the six arts.

During the Shang and Zhou periods, the military made use of martial dances (a type of drill that utilized weapons) to train soldiers and boost morale. Soldiers were armed with weapons in neatly lined-up formations while dancing in wild and rough movements, giving out a dominating power.

During the feudal conflicting for hegemony in the Spring and Autumn

六艺

中国古代儒家要求学生掌握的六种基本才能，即礼、乐、射、御、书、数，被称为"六艺"。礼，指礼仪、品德；乐，指音乐、诗歌、舞蹈等；射，指射箭技术；御，指驾驭马车的技术；书，指识字、书写能力；数，指算术。

Six Arts

Confucians in ancient China required students to master six basic skills, which were rituals, music, archery, charioteering, mathematics and calligraphy. These skills were known as the Six Arts. The art of rituals meant etiquette and moral character. The art of music included music, poetry and dance. Archery referred to archery techniques. Charioteering was concerned with the skills of controlling chariots. Calligraphy referred to literacy and the ability to write. Mathematics had to do with numbers.

221），诸侯争霸，各国都很重视士兵的身体素质训练，并开展了相应的武艺教习。如齐国每年都要举行春秋两季的"角试"（一种比武形式），来选拔豪杰英雄充实到军队当中。魏国的武卒选拔十分严格，被选中者要进行相应的武术训练。

在读书人中间，也讲究军事武艺的训练。孔子的弟子子路和冉有就有着逼人的武风。一次，孔子与几位弟子在山野中漫步，孔子问弟子们都有什么志愿。子路回答说，他的志向是在国家危难之时，手持

Period and the Warring States Period (770 B.C.-221 B.C.), each state paid great attention to the physical fitness training of their soldiers and consequently extended the teaching and learning of relevant martial arts. In the State of Qi, for example, *Jue Shi* (a form of martial arts contest) was held every spring

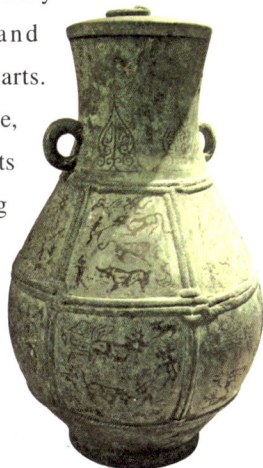

• 狩猎纹铜壶（春秋）
Hunting-patterned Copper Kettle (the Spring and Autumn Period, 770 B.C.-476B.C.)

武术
Chinese Martial Arts

- 战国铜器纹饰中的射箭场面
Archery Scene Depicted on a Bronze Pattern from the
Warring States Period (475 B.C.-221 B.C.)

- 宴乐射猎攻战纹壶【局部】(战国)
Kettle with Patterns of Banquet, Archery,
Hunting, and Warring [Partial] (Warring
States Period, 475 B.C.-221 B.C.)

and autumn in order to single out heroic figures to join and enrich the military. In the State of Wei, the selection of warriors was very strict. The selected ones had to undergo relevant martial arts training.

Trainings on military martial arts were also stressed among literati. Even Confucius' disciples, Zilu and Ranyou, were winged with impressive martial styles. There was a time when Confucius was going on a walk in the mountains with a few disciples and he asked them about their ambitions. Zilu replied that his ambition was to use his halberd to fight along with other soldiers in the battlefield to eliminate the enemy when

长戟，与将士们一同驰骋疆场，消灭强敌。孔子的另一个弟子冉有是个运筹帷幄的将帅之才，曾率领鲁国军队与齐国作战，打败齐军。在战场上，他手持长矛，身先士卒，冲锋陷阵，勇猛无敌。

这一时期还开始盛行佩剑与论剑之风，剑的制造及剑术都得到了空前的发展。此时还出现了游侠（古时豪爽好交游、轻生重义、勇

the country was in danger. Confucius' other disciple, Ranyou, with the talent of being a general, once led the army of the State of Lu in the war against the Qi State and defeated the Qi army. On the battlefield, he carried a long spear, took the lead in the charge and demonstrated his unrivaled bravery.

This period also saw the beginning of the prevalent fashion of sword carrying and sword discussions. Sword

孔子

孔子（前551—前479），姓孔，名丘，字仲尼，中国古代思想家、教育家、政治家，儒家的创始人。相传曾修《诗》、《书》，订《礼》、《乐》，序《周易》，撰《春秋》。他一生从事传道、授业、解惑，被尊为"至圣先师，万世师表"。后人将孔子及其弟子的言行和思想记录下来，作成《论语》。

孔子提出有教无类、因材施教的教育思想，认为无论贫富贵贱，人人都享有平等受教育的权利。每个人在志趣、能力等方面有差异，应根据学生的具体情况进行不同的教育。孔子提倡"仁"、"礼"，"仁"包含做人的一切美德，主张"仁者爱人"。"礼"是要求人们加强个人修养，时刻约束自己，各种言行要符合社会道德规范。

Confucius

Confucius (551 B.C.-479 B.C.), surnamed Kong with the first name of Qiu and a courtesy name of Zhongni, was an ancient Chinese thinker, educator, politician, and the

● 孔子像
Statue of Confucius

founder of Confucianism. It is said that he had proofread *The Book of Poetry* and *The Book of History*, revised *The Book of Rites* and *The Book of Classic Music*, prefaced *The Book of Changes*, and composed *Spring and Autumn Annals*. His whole life was devoted to preaching the Tao (a universal law), imparting knowledge and solving doubts. He was revered as a "venerable sage and a teacher for all ages". His words, teachings and conduct were all recorded in *The Analects of Confucius*.

Confucius proposed the ideas of providing education for all people without discrimination, and teaching students according to their individual aptitude. He believed that everyone should enjoy equal rights to education regardless of wealth or social status. Differences exist among people in people's individual interest and ability, so different ways of education should be implemented according to the student's specific circumstances. Confucius advocated "benevolence" and "propriety". Benevolence includes all the virtues of man and is embodied in his proposition that "a benevolent one gives love to others." Propriety requires people to strengthen their personal integrity and to hold them in self-control at all times so that all their words and deeds will comply with social ethics.

于排难解纷的人），武技的社会功能性开始向多样化发展。

秦始皇（前259—前210）统一六国，建立秦王朝，收天下之兵，聚于咸阳，实际上是在民间实行禁武。当时民间虽然禁武，但军队中的习武活动仍蓬勃发展。陕西西安秦始皇陵兵马俑坑，像一座规

manufacturing and swordsmanship also acquired unprecedented development. Wandering swordsmen (known as *You Xia*, the unrestrained and open-minded individuals who enjoyed making friends, attached more importance to propriety than life itself and were ready to help others) also appeared around this time. The social function of martial arts began

• 青铜古剑（战国）
Bronze Sword (Warring States Period, 475 B.C.-221 B.C.)

模庞大的地下军事博物馆，向世
人展示了秦代在军事方面的巨大
成就。

to diversify.

When the First Emperor of Qin (259 B.C.-210 B.C.) unified all the seven states and created the Qin Dynasty, all weapons across the country were demanded to be gathered in Xianyang, capital of the Qin Dynasty. It was actually a move to ban martial arts in the civil society. Although martial arts were banned in the civil society at that time, they continued to flourish within the army. The vaults of the terracotta warriors and horses unearthed from the mausoleum of the First Qin Emperor in Xi'an of northwest China's Shaanxi Province are like a large underground military museum, which exposed the great achievements of the Qin Dynasty to the world.

• 秦始皇像
Statue of the First Emperor of Qin

兵马俑坑

兵马俑坑是秦始皇陵的陪葬坑，位于陵园东侧，有"世界第八奇迹"之誉。已经发掘的三个兵马俑坑是秦国军队的缩影，一号坑为右军，二号坑为左军，三号坑是指挥部。三个兵马俑坑共出土了八千多个陶俑，有步兵、骑兵、战车等兵种，陶俑身披铠甲，威风凛凛。还有数百匹陶马、百余辆战车，以及大量青铜兵器等文物。

The Vaults of Terracotta Warriors and Horses

The vaults of the terracotta warriors and horses are the accompanying burial vaults for the mausoleum of the First Emperor of Qin. The vaults are located in the east side of the mausoleum yard and hold the reputation as "the eighth wonder of the world". Three terracotta vaults have already been excavated, but they are only an epitome of the Qin army. Vault One was the right army, Vault Two was the left army, and Vault Three was the commanding headquarter. Over 8,000 terracotta figures of infantry, cavalry, chariot and other branches of the military were excavated from the three terracotta vaults. The terracotta figures are draped with armors, and appear in awe-inspiring stances. Hundreds of ceramic horses, more than 100 combat chariots and a large amount of bronze weapons were also excavated together with other artifacts.

兵马俑（秦）
Terracotta Warriors and Horses (Qin Dynasty, 221 B.C.—206 B.C.)

秦代，民间盛行起角抵戏，是一种以摔跤、拳斗为基础的，有故事情节和配乐的武打娱乐活动。这大大促进了武艺的表演、竞技和娱乐功能的发展。

秦汉以来，在宴会场合形成了"宴乐兴舞"的习俗，以及盛行角抵、击剑以及手持器械的舞练。中国历史上著名的"鸿门宴"中的"项庄舞剑，意在沛公"，便是这一形式的反映。此外，还有"刀舞"，"力舞"等，虽具娱乐性，但从技术上更近于今天套路形式的运动。

During the Qin Dynasty (221 B.C.-206 B.C.), wrestling matches became popular in the civil society. It was a martial art activity based on wrestling and fist fighting in the form of entertainment accompanied by a storyline and music. It greatly promoted the development of performances of martial arts as well as its athletics and entertaining functions.

Since the Qin and Han Dynasties, the custom of "banquet dance" had been formed on banquet occasions, together with the prevalent dancing drills of wrestling, sword-fighting and handheld weapons. A typical example of that was reflected in the famous story of Hongmen Feast in Chinese history, in which *Xiang Zhuang performed the sword dance in order to conceal his attempt to take Pei's life*. Beyond that, there was also the "blade dance", "power dance" and the like, which might have the function of entertainment, but were technically much closer to the routine exercises of today.

● 木篦上的《角抵图》（秦）
Wrestling Picture on a Wooden Comb (Qin Dynasty, 221 B.C.-206 B.C.)

项庄舞剑，意在沛公

据司马迁（约前145或前135—？）所著的《史记·项羽本纪》记载，公元前206年，在秦都城咸阳外的鸿门，两支抗秦部队的首领项羽和刘邦举行了一次宴会，史称"鸿门宴"。席间项羽麾下的武将项庄在酒席上拔剑起舞，为宴会助兴，实际上意图乘机刺杀刘邦。项羽叔父项伯看出项庄的意图，也拔剑起舞，掩护刘邦，使刘邦得以脱身，这就是典故"项庄舞剑，意在沛公"的出处。

● 《鸿门宴图》（汉）
Picture of Hongmen Feast (Han Dynasty, 206 B.C.- 220 A.D.)

Xiang Zhuang's Sword Dance and His Attempt on Pei's Life

According to *The Journey of Xiang Yu* in *Records of the Grand Historian* by Sima Qian (approx. 145 or 135 B.C. -?), two leaders of the militaries against the Qin Dynasty, Xiang Yu and Liu Bang, held a banquet at Hongmen outside of Xianyang, the capital of Qin in 206 B.C.. This banquet was historically known as the Hongmen Feast. During the banquet, a general, Xiang Zhuang, under the command of Xiang Yu, drew out his sword and started to perform a sword dance in order to add fun to the banquet. In actuality, it was intended as an opportunity to assassinate Liu Bang. Xiang Bo, Xiang Yu's uncle, who discerned Xiang Zhuang's intention, also drew out his sword and performed the sword dance to cover Liu Bang and help him escape. This is the source of the classical allusion of *Xiang Zhuang's sword dance and his attempt on Pei's life*.

虞姬

- **虞姬像**

  虞姬是项羽之妃，长得很美，又善于剑舞。楚汉之战，项羽被困，兵孤粮尽。虞姬深夜在帐中为项羽拔剑起舞。为了打消项羽的后顾之忧，让他从容对敌，虞姬舞罢自刎。

  Portrait of Yuji

  Yuji was Xiang Yu's concubine who was quite beautiful and very good at sword dance as well. In the battle between Chu and Han, Xiang Yu was trapped in the situation that his soldiers were isolated and the food supply was depleted. Late one night, Yuji drew the sword to perform sword dancing for him in the tent. In order to free Xiang Yu from worries for her future so that he could calmly face the enemies, Yuji took her own life after the dance.

汉代是中国封建社会中一个辉煌的时代。在长达百年的与匈奴的战争中，汉朝对军事的依赖更直接促进了军队和民间对武术的重视。射箭在战争中仍起着重要作用，汉代涌现了大批神箭手，流传下来许多关于神箭手的传奇故事。其中最有名的是"李广射虎"的故事。李广是汉武帝（前156－前87）手下的一员大将，身材高大威猛，练就了一身好武艺，善于骑射。有一次，李广夜间巡逻，突然发现草丛中蜷

The Han Dynasty (206 B.C.- 220 A.D.) was a glorious era of the Chinese feudal society. In the century-long war against the Huns, the Han Dynasty's dependence on the military directly contributed to the emphasis on martial arts both in the military and in civilian society. Archery continued to play an important role in wars and a large number of marksmen in archery were produced. Among the legendary stories of master archers that have been handed down, one of the most famous is the story of Li Guang Shooting the Tiger. Li Guang (?-119 B.C.) was a general under Emperor Wu

● 李广像
Portrait of Li Guang

● 铁镞(汉)
Iron Arrowhead (Han Dynasty, 206 B.C.-220 A.D.)

● 盘龙纹柄铜剑(汉)
Bronze Sword with Dragon-patterned Handle (Han Dynasty, 206 B.C.- 220 A.D.)

- 《狩猎放牧图》画像砖（汉）

  在汉代画像砖（石）上刻有狩猎、比武图，展现了当时的武术技艺。

  Brick Painting of *Hunting and Herding* (Han Dynasty, 206 B.C.- 220 A.D.)

  Pictures of hunting and martial art contests were engraved onto the bricks (stones) from the Han Dynasty, where martial arts of that time were depicted.

伏着一个黑影，似动非动。他以为是一只老虎，便张弓一箭射去。天亮后，他派士兵前去查看，发现原来射中的是一块巨石，箭已深深地射进石头，可见其力大惊人。

到了三国时期（220—280），手搏、击剑、射箭等实用技艺长盛不衰。刀逐渐取代了剑在军事舞台上的地位，剑逐渐转移至非军事用途并继续发展，刀剑之术以及相扑、角抵等活动开始东传日本。

两晋、南北朝是中国历史上剧烈动荡的时代，也是中华各民族

of the Han Dynasty. He was tall, mighty, well-trained in martial arts, and versed in shooting on horseback. One night, Li Guang was patrolling when he suddenly spied a dark figure crouched in the grass. Assuming it was a tiger, he quickly shot an arrow at it. After dawn, he dispatched some soldiers to check out on the tiger, but they discovered that what he shot was but a boulder. They also found that the arrow had deeply penetrated the stone, though. It was thus proved what an astonishing power Li Guang had.

With the arrival of the Three Kingdom Period (220-280), such practical skills as bare-hand combat, sword fighting, archery and others became ever-prospering. *Dao* (blades or broadswords) gradually replaced swords in the military arena, while swords gradually shifted to use for non-military purposes and continued to develop. Meanwhile, sword techniques, sumo, wrestling and others began to spread eastward to Japan.

During the period of both the Eastern and Western Jin Dynasties (265-420) and the Southern and Northern Dynasties (420-589), China had seen an era of intense turbulences in history and a period of the great ethnic integration in China. The national integration injected new blood into the Chinese culture

武术的起源、发展 Origin and Development of Martial Arts

● 《车马出行图》画像砖（南朝）

Brick Painting of *Tour on Horses and Wagons* (Southern Dynasty, 420-589)

大融合的时期。民族融合为中华文化注入了新鲜的血液，也使中国武术有了较大发展。两晋政权建立不过三十年，统治阶层的八位王侯之间就为争夺统治权而爆发了"八王之乱"。匈奴、鲜卑、羯、氐、羌等西北民族也纷纷进入中原，相互混战，先后建立十余个政权，史称"十六国"。这一时期，战乱频繁，战争促进了军事武艺的发展，特别是民族间的战争，使得各民族的武艺得到了发展与交流。偏居于长江流域的汉族政权多崇尚享乐苟安，过着声色玩乐的生活，但这在一定程度上促进了武术娱乐功能的发展。不过并非人们都醉生梦死，贪图享乐，像"闻鸡起舞"的祖

and enabled Chinese martial arts to undergo considerable development. Within 30 years of the establishment, the Eastern and Western Jin Dynasties fell to the outbreak of the Upheaval of Eight Princes, where the eight princes in the ruling class fought each other for the right to rule. Northwestern tribes such as the Huns, Xianbei, Jie, Di, and Qiang successively invaded the Central Plains, aroused confusion and warfare and created more than a dozen political powers in succession, known as the Sixteen States. During this period, wars promoted the development of the military and martial arts, and inter-tribal wars, in particular, enabled the development and exchange of martial arts among various ethnic groups. The political power held by the ethnic Han, residing in the Yangtze River basin, was inclined for enjoyment and temporary ease and indulged in various joys of life. To some extent, however, this helped promote the development of martial arts in their function as an entertainment. However, not everyone was leading a befuddled

• 《射猎图》（魏晋南北朝）
Picture of Archery and Hunting (Wei, Jin, Southern and Northern Dynasties, 220-589)

逖、刘琨，就发奋练武，重振武风。南北朝时，佛教、道教等宗教迅速发展，使武术与宗教活动有了较多的联系，对中国武术的发展起了重要作用的少林寺就是在当时建立的。此时武术向多功能发展，不仅具有习武的功能，还有健身及表演的功能。

life of pleasure-seeking. People like Zu Ti and Liu Kun, who "rose to exercise with the sword upon hearing the crows of roosters", were determined to train themselves in martial arts and revive the power of the martial arts. During the Southern and Northern Dynasties, the rapid development of religion like Buddhism, Taoism and others allowed for a connection between martial arts and religious activities. The *Shaolin Temple*, which played a profound role in the development of Chinese martial arts, was established at this time. During this period, martial arts was developing into a multi-functional practice that involved not only the learning of martial arts, but also the functions of fitness and performances.

• 《射猎图》画像砖（魏晋）
Brick Painting of *Archery and Hunting* (Wei and Jin Dynasties, 220-420)

闻鸡起舞

　　祖逖是个胸怀坦荡、具有远大抱负的人。他与幼时好友刘琨感情深厚，还有着共同的远大理想：建功立业，复兴国家，成为栋梁之才。一次，半夜里祖逖在睡梦中听到公鸡的鸣叫声，就把刘琨喊醒，说："咱们以后听见鸡叫就起床练剑如何？"刘琨欣然同意。于是他们每天鸡叫后起床练剑。春去冬来，寒来暑往，从没有间断过。功夫不负有心人，经过长期的刻苦学习和训练，他们二人终于成为能文能武的全才，实现了报效国家的愿望。

Rise Upon Hearing Rooster Crows to Exercise with the Sword

Zu Ti was an open-minded and ambitious person. He and his close friend since childhood, Liu Kun, shared the same lofty ideal: to make contributions and accomplishments to revive their own country, the Jin, and become the backbones of the country. One night when Zu Ti heard the crows of a rooster in his sleep, he woke Liu Kun up and said to him: "From now on, why don't we get up on hearing the crows of the rooster and practice with our swords?" Liu Kan readily agreed. From then on, they woke up every morning to the crow of the roosters and practiced their swordsmanship. From spring to winter, year in year out, their practice was never interrupted. After quite a long period of study and training, their hard work finally paid off. They became versatile individuals well versed in both the literary and martial arts, and finally realized their hope to serve the country.

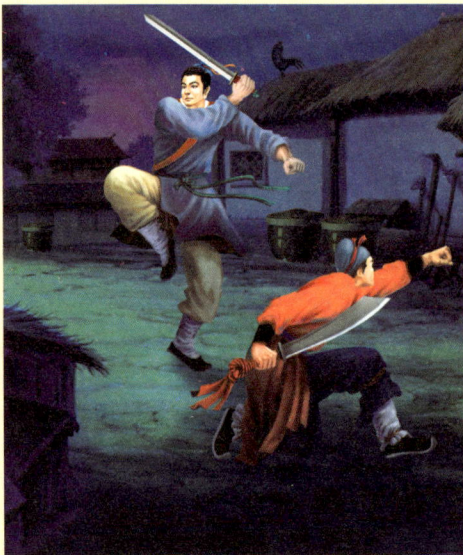

● 闻鸡起舞
Rise upon Hearing Rooster Crows to Exercise with the Sword

《仪卫出行图》（北齐）

Picture of the Procession of Guards of Honor (Northern Qi Dynasty, 550-577)

隋代（581—618）结束了中国数百年分裂割据的局面，建立了较完备的国家政权。随后，唐代随承隋制而加以完备。唐代（618—907）文化是一种开放的文化，中外文化交流相当普遍。武术文化在这一时期得到了很大发展。外来文化丰富了传统文化的内容，不单是武舞、弓射、摔跤等活动，乃至于整个唐代的重武风习中都有外来文

The Sui Dynasty (581-618) concluded the century-long period of chaotic division in China, and established a much-accomplished national entity. After that, the Tang Dynasty inherited all the systems of the Sui Dynasty and made them more perfect. The culture of the Tang Dynasty (618-907) was an open one in which Sino-foreign cultural exchanges were quite common. The culture of martial arts in this period also achieved great development. The enrichment that the foreign culture brought to the contents of the traditional culture was not limited in such activities as martial dances, archery and wrestling, but could be traced in the overall emphasis that the Tang Dynasty had placed upon martial arts practice. The Tang Dynasty also initiated the martial art examination system, which served to single out individuals talented with the feat of martial arts by means of tests. The creation of the martial arts examination system was the most important event in the history of martial arts, and played a prominent part in promoting the development of martial arts. The examination system gave people the possibility to obtain official positions through the practice of martial arts, which greatly inspired people's enthusiasm

化的痕迹。唐代开始实行武举制，以考试选拔武技人才。武举制的创立是中国武术史上最重要的事件，对武术的发展起了促进作用。武举制使人们看到了以武入仕的可能，激发了人们的习武热情。隋唐时期器械武艺得到了迅速发展，如刀、枪、剑、棍、弓、弩等器械武艺可谓千名万状；角抵、剑舞、矛舞等形式更是丰富多彩。

for martial arts. The martial art of weapons in the Sui and Tang Dynasties also achieved rapid development, as techniques in blades, spears, swords, staffs, bows and crossbows came in various styles. Wrestling, sword dancing and spear dancing were also flourished in rich varieties.

During the reign of the Song Dynasty (960-1279), the long-term confrontation with minority regimes such as the Liao

• 持盾武士陶俑(隋)
Terracotta Figure of Shielded Warrior (Sui Dynasty, 581-618)

• 青瓷武士俑(唐)
Porcelain Figure of Warrior (Tang Dynasty, 618-907)

• 狩猎纹铜镜（唐）
Bronze Mirror with Hunting Pattern
(Tang Dynasty, 618-907)

• 狩猎纹铜镜上的纹饰（唐）
Decorative Pattern of Hunting on a
Bronze Mirror (Tang Dynasty, 618-907)

　　宋朝（960—1279）统治期间，与辽(907—1125)、金（1115—1234）、西夏（1038—1227）等少数民族政权长期对峙，民族矛盾、阶级矛盾十分尖锐。由于这一时期战争频繁，宋朝统治者十分重视武备，军队实行募兵制，通过选募、武举考试选拔武艺人才；军事训练采用统一教法，并制定统一的考核标准。军事训练规范化、系统化促进了武艺的提高。这一时期兵器的种类大增，各种兵器武艺争相竞赛。民间练武活动蓬勃兴起，出现了浪迹江湖，以习武卖艺为生的"路歧人"。武术演练形式不仅有单练，还有对练。民间自发组织起了各种武术团体，如

(907-1125), the Jin (1115-1234) and the Western Xia (1038-1227) had created sharp ethnic conflicts as well as class contradictions. Due to the frequent wars in this period, rulers of the Song Dynasty attached great importance to military preparations. An enlisting system was implemented in the military, and martial art talents were selected through both the enlistment and the martial arts examination system. Military trainings had a unified method of teaching as well as unified standards for evaluation. The standardized and systematized military training further promoted the enhancement of martial arts. The variety of weapons in this period also increased greatly, and martial arts techniques

• 《中兴四将图》 刘松年（宋）
Portraits of Four Generals for National Revival by
Liu Songnian (Song Dynasty, 960-1279)

"角抵社"、"相扑社"、"弓箭社"等。民间武术团体的出现，进一步推动了民间武艺的发展。随着商业的繁荣，城市中出现了游艺场所"勾栏"、"瓦舍"，专门进行各种武艺表演，把武术列为表演项目，统称"百戏"。武术体系在宋代基本形成。除了对抗性的角抵、手搏外，套子武艺（一种以武术套路为主要表演形式的武艺）有了较大的发展，奠定了中国古代武术的基本格局。武术自此基本摆脱了从属于军事训练的地位，在民间广阔的土壤中生长起来，并按自身的规律演进。

based upon these weapons spurred in competition against each other. Martial arts activities in the civil sector thrived as well. There were individuals who wandered about all corners of the country in search for worthy foes, as well as street performers, called *Lu Qi* (wandering) people, who performed martial arts to make a living. As for the drill forms for martial arts, there were not only single-person drills, but also pair-up drills. In the civilian society, people organized various martial arts groups by themselves, such as the "wrestling society", the "*Xiang Pu* (sumo) society", the "archery society", and the like. The emergence of martial

arts groups in the civil sector provided further impetus for the development of martial arts in the civilian society. As commercial businesses thrived, entertainment venues such as the *Gou Lan* (hooked columns) and *Wa She* (tiled house) also appeared in cities, and were dedicated to a variety of martial arts performances. Martial arts performances were categorized in these places as one of their program items, collectively known as the *Bai Xi* (acrobatics). Basically, the system of martial arts had been established in the Song Dynasty. In addition to the confrontational wrestling and bare-hand grappling, formula martial arts, called *Tao Zi Wu Yi* (a type of martial arts routine utilized mainly as a performance style), was also developed greatly. It laid a basic pattern for Chinese ancient martial arts. Since then, martial arts gradually broke away from its attachment to military training and grounded its growth in the soil of the vast civil sector. It has thus developed in accordance with its own law of evolution.

• 挂剑武官石刻像(宋)
Rock Carving of a Military Officer Leaning on a Sword (Song Dynasty, 907-1279)

《水浒传》

　　《水浒传》是中国历史上第一部用白话文写成的长篇章回小说，是中国四大名著之一，流传极广，脍炙人口。此书作于元末明初，作者施耐庵根据民间流传的北宋末年宋江起义传奇加工而成。全书讲述了北宋末年官逼民反，以宋江为首的108位英雄好汉在梁山泊聚众起义的故事。再现了封建时代农民起义从发生、发展到失败的全过程。《水浒传》的故事发生在北宋末年，社会动荡不安，战争频繁，出于保家卫国、自卫防身的需要，民间尚武风气盛行，出现了练武组织。《水浒传》中的108位英雄大多是农民出身，武艺高强，侠肝义胆，为除暴安良、反抗朝廷压迫而聚义。《水浒传》故事情节曲折、语言生动，塑造了宋江、李逵、武松、林冲、鲁智深等性格鲜明的英雄形象，有很高的艺术价值。

• 《水浒传》中的战斗场面
Scene of Battlefield in
Outlaws of the Marsh

Outlaws of the Marsh

Outlaws of the Marsh is the first chapter novel ever written in vernacular language in the history of China. As one of the four Chinese masterpieces, it is very widely-spread and well talked about in everyone's mouth. The book was composed in the late Yuan and early Ming Dynasties by Shi Nai'an, who based his novel on the legends and folklores of the Song Jiang uprising in the late Northern Song Dynasty (960-1127). The novel tells about the cruel rule of the government, which gave rise to the consequent revolts that occurred in the late Northern Song Dynasty. Song Jiang led 107 heroes and gathered at Liangshanpo in revolts. The novel reproduced the entire process of a peasant uprising in a feudal era from its beginning through the development to the eventual failure. The background of *Outlaws of the Marsh* was cast in the late Northern Song Dynasty when social unrest prevailed and frequent wars occurred. For the sake of self-defense and protection for the homeland, martial arts became rampant in civilian societies and martial arts organizations came into being. The majority of the 108 heroes in *Outlaws of the Marsh* had a low origin of peasanthood but phenomenal feats of martial arts and upright character of magnanimity. They banded together and utilized their physical prowess to weed out the cruel, pacify the good and revolt against oppression from the imperial court. The twist-and-turn storyline and the vivid language utilized in *Outlaws of the Marsh* shaped out the heroic image of such characters as Song Jiang, Li Kui, Wu Song, Lin Chong and Lu Zhisheng. It is a literary work of highly artistic values.

十三世纪初，中国北部的蒙古民族兴起，在成吉思汗领导下，建立起蒙古汗国。至忽必烈时，灭南宋，建立统一南北的大帝国元朝（1279—1368）。元朝的建立，促进了民族的融合与文化交流，少数民族富有特色的武艺技能对武术发展有着特殊的贡献。

明代（1368—1644）时的武术

In the early 13th century, the Mongolian tribe in northern China rose under the leadership of Genghis Khan and established the Mongol Empire. By the time of the reign of Khubilai Khan, the Southern Song had been destroyed and replaced by the Yuan Dynasty (1279-1368), which unified the north and south of China. The establishment of the Yuan Dynasty pushed forward

• 《胡人出猎图》【局部】（明）张龙章
Barbarians Hunting [Partial] (Ming Dynasty, 1368-1644) By Zhang Longzhang

• 元代士兵像
Portrait of a Soldier from the Yuan Dynasty (1279-1368)

不再仅以刀、枪、棍分门别类，而是在全国范围内形成了诸多风格迥异的流派，十八般武艺在明代也有了具体的名称和内容。明代不但拳法众多，而且器械套路也更加丰富多彩，开始有势有法，有拳谱有歌诀。这说明脱胎于军事格斗技术的武术，在此时已逐步形成以套路为主的运动形式，并远远超过对抗性运动的发展。

明代武术的大发展与明太祖

the national integration and cultural exchange. Some of the distinctive martial arts skills introduced by the ethnic minorities made special contributions to the development of martial arts.

The martial arts in the Ming Dynasty (1368-1644) were no longer classified in the categories of blades, spears and staffs. Instead, there were many schools of martial arts with disparate styles emerging all over the country. The term of Eighteen Techniques of Chinese Martial Arts was thereupon established

明代士兵像
Portrait of a Soldier from the Ming Dynasty
(1368-1644)

朱元璋重视文武全才的理念分不开。他主张"武官习礼仪，文人学骑射"。当时出现了一大批既是军队将领又为武术发展做出卓越贡献的人物。武术及军事著作在明代大量出现，如唐顺之的《武编》、俞大猷的《正气堂集》、戚继光的《纪效新书》《练兵实纪》、何良臣的《阵纪》、郑若曾的《江南经略》、茅元仪的《武备志》等一批武术及军事名著，就是由军事训练

with its formal usage and concrete contents during the Ming Dynasty. There were not only numerous *Quan Fa* (fist techniques) in the Ming Dynasty, but also rich varieties in weapon techniques and drill patterns. Different trends and rules emerged in martial arts and various *Quan Pu* (manuals of fist technique training) and *Ge Jue* (formulas in verses) were composed as well. This signified that the martial arts taken away from its original military context had gradually materialized at this time in a form of sports focused essentially on *Tao Lu* (form, or drill patterns)— a development well beyond the form of mere confrontational sports.

The tremendous development of martial arts in the Ming Dynasty could not have been achieved without the concept of full literary and martial capacity upheld by Zhu Yuanzhang, the founding emperor of Taizu of the Ming Dynasty. He advocated the idea that "military officers should learn etiquette, while scholars should learn riding and shooting." There were waves of personages who not only served as military commanding generals but also made outstanding contributions to the

• 戚继光画像
Portrait of Qi Jiguang

• 《武备志》中弩的使用
Usage of Crossbow as Described in
Treatise on Military Preparations

及战争实践的经验总结而产生，为后世研究武术提供了重要依据。明代与日本的文化交流频繁、广泛。日本刀法深受中国武术家关注，而中国武术在这一时期深刻影响了日本柔道和空手道的创立。

清朝（1644—1911）统治时期，由于贵族为维持自己的统治地位，一度限制练武，所以清代的武术活动不如明代繁盛。但由于武术在民间已有广泛群众基础，加之当时存在许多反清复明组织，习武练

development of martial arts. A large quantity of writings and masterpieces about martial arts and military affairs appeared at this time, such as Tang Shunzhi's *Wu Bian* (*Martial Arts Compilation*), Yu Dayou's *Zheng Qi Tang Ji* (*Collection at the Zhengqi Hall*), Qi Jiguang's *Ji Xiao Xin Shu* (*New Book Recording Effective Techniques*) and *Lian Bing Shi Ji* (*Records of Military Training*), He Liangchen's *Zhen Ji* (*Array Records*), Zheng Ruoceng's *Jiang Nan Jing Lüe* (*Jiangnan Management and Plans*), and Mao Yuanyi's *Wu Bei Zhi*

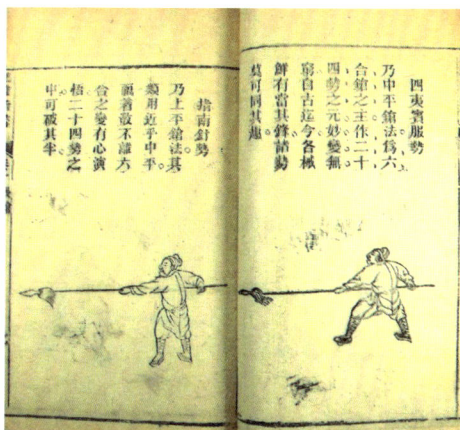

• 《纪效新书》书影
Photo of *New Book Recording Effective Techniques*

(*Treatise on Military Preparations*). These resulted from the examination and summarization of military trainings and practices of warfare provided an important basis for later studies of martial arts. Since the Ming Dynasty had frequent and extensive cultural exchanges with Japan, the Japanese blade styles caught the attention of Chinese martial artists. On the other hand, Chinese martial arts during this time exerted profound effects on the creation of judo and karate in Japan.

During the reign of the Qing Dynasty (1644-1911), in order to maintain their ruling power, the noble class had once put a ban on martial arts practice. That's why the martial arts activities in the Qing Dynasty were not as active as they were in the Ming Dynasty. However, due to the mass base for martial arts rooted in the civil sector as well as the existence of some organizations committed to overthrowing the Qing Dynasty and

• 古代建筑上的《狩猎图》
Picture of Hunting on an Ancient Architecture

功以图推翻清朝统治，反而使各种流派的武术更加纷呈于世。以地区分有南派、北派；以山川分有少林派、武当派、峨眉派、崂山派等；以门类分有太极、形意、八卦，以及长拳和短打等。武术流派林立，象征着武术事业的兴旺发达。

武术
Chinese Martial Arts

reinstating the Ming Dynasty by resorting to the practice of martial arts, different styles and schools of martial arts were spawned in the country. In terms of geographic division, there were the southern school and the northern school. According to the mountains and rivers where they were based, there were the *Shaolin* style, *Wudang* style, *Emei* style, *Laoshan* style and so on. Pertaining to the schools, they were classified as *Tai Chi*, *Xing Yi*, *Ba Gua*, *Chang Quan* (long-range fist technique) and *Duan Da* (short-range fight), among others. The multitude of different martial arts styles and schools signified the prosperity and growth of the martial arts industry.

> 近现代武术的传承

　　到了近代，武术适应时代的变化，逐步成为中国近代体育的组成部分。民国时期（1912—1949），武术被作为一种强国健体的教育手段推向学校，列为正式课程。在一些运动会上，武术还被列为竞赛项目。民间出现了许多拳社、武士会等武术组织，其中有两个影响最为深远的武术团体：一个是霍元甲于1910年创立的精武体育会，另一个是张之江于1927年在南京成立的中央国术馆。1923年在上海举办了中华武术大会，1936年中国武术队曾赴柏林奥运会进行表演。

　　1949年中华人民共和国成立后，武术作为一项优秀的民族文化遗产得到了继承和发展。国家不但在高等师范院校及体育学院开设了

> Heritage of Modern and Contemporary Martial Arts

When it comes to modern times as martial arts adapted to the changes of the times, it has gradually become an integral part of modern physical education. During the Republic of China period (1912-1949), martial arts was introduced into schools as a means of education to enhance the national power and physical strength and was listed as formal curricula. In some sports events, martial arts was also listed as an event. In the civil sector, there emerged many martial arts organizations like boxing communities, warrior societies and others, of which the two most influential martial arts organizations were the *Jingwu* Athletic Association, founded by Huo Yuanjia in 1910, and the Central *Guoshu* Academy established in Nanjing by Zhang Zhijiang in 1927. The Chinese Martial Arts Tournament was

● 霍元甲
Huo Yuanjia

武术专业，还组织专业人员在继承传统拳术的基础上，广泛吸取众家之长，整理出简化太极拳、初级长拳、中级长拳以及器械套路。1957年，武术第一次被列为正式比赛项目。1958年，中国武术协会成立，《武术竞赛规则》、《武术运动员技术等级标准》、《竞赛规定套路》、《中国武术段位制》等相继制定颁布。2009年国家体育总局规定了武术的概念：武术是以中华文化为理论基础，以技击方法为基本内容，以套路、格斗、功法为主要运动形式的传统体育。中国武术源

held in 1923 in Shanghai. In 1936, the Chinese Martial Arts Team was invited to demonstrate their art at the Berlin Olympics.

After the founding of the People's Republic of China in 1949, as an extraordinary item of national cultural legacy, martial arts secured inheritance and further development. The state not only established martial arts as a special major in advanced normal universities and physical education institutes, but also organized professional personnel to widely absorb the strong points of various schools and work out the simplified version of *Tai Chi Quan*, intermediate *Chang Quan*, preliminary *Chang Quan* as well as weapon drill patterns on the basis of traditional martial arts. Martial arts was first listed as an official competition category in 1957. When the Chinese Martial Arts Association was founded in 1958, such provisions as the Martial Arts Competition Rules, Standard Technical Grades for Martial Arts Athletes, Designated Drill Patterns in Competition, Chinese Martial Arts Ranking System and others were successively formulated and promulgated. In 2009, the General Administration of Sport defined the concept of martial arts as a traditional

physical training which features Chinese culture as its theoretical basis, encompasses fighting skills as its basic contents, and adopts drill patterns, fist fighting and exercise techniques as its primary form of exercises. Chinese martial arts has had a long history dating back to antiquity, and through the process of its development and practice over time, it has formed unique national styles and features. As a national art and cultural treasure, martial arts has been deeply loved by Chinese people and well-accepted by international friends.

远流长，在发展演进过程中，经过长期的实践，形成了独特的民族风格和特点。武术作为中国的国术，不但深受国人喜爱，而且也受到国际友人的青睐。

中国武术在海外

中国武术的影响极为广泛，最早是传到日本和东南亚一带。据记载，明代拳师陈元赟东渡日本，传授少林拳法，奠定了日本柔道的基础。日本的空手道、合气道，朝鲜的跆拳道，泰国的暹罗拳，菲律宾的棍术都不同程度地受到中国武术的影响。现今中国武术已风靡世界，其所具有的健身、技击、艺术欣赏等综合功能，越来越吸引国外的武术爱好者。美国成立了"全美中国武术协会"，芝加哥、纽约、旧金山等城市还成立了"少林功夫学校"。"功夫"、"少林"、"太极"、"武术"的汉语拼音——"*Gong Fu*"（Kung Fu）、"*Shao Lin*"、"*Tai Chi*"、"*Wu Shu*"已成为英语中的常用词。

Chinese Martial Arts Overseas

Chinese Martial Arts has wielded extremely wide influences. The earliest influence of Chinese martial arts was felt in Japan and Southeast Asia. According to records, Master Chen Yuanyun from the Ming Dynasty traveled to Japan, where he taught *Shaolin* fist techniques and laid down the foundation for Japanese Judo. In a sense, Japanese Karate and Aikido, Korean Taekwondo, Siam boxing in Thailand, and the cudgel play in Philippines were all influenced by Chinese martial arts in varying degrees. Nowadays, Chinese martial arts has overwhelmed the world. Its unique features, which incorporate such functions as fitness, fighting skills and artistic appreciation have attracted more and more foreign enthusiasts for martial arts. The Chinese Martial Arts Association in America was established in the United States, and *Shaolin Kungfu* Schools were founded in Chicago, New York, San Francisco and other cities. Such words based on the Chinese phonetic system of *pinyin* as *Gong Fu*, *Shao Lin*, *Tai Chi* and *Wu Shu* have become commonly used vocabulary in English.

武术的著名门派
Famous Sects and Schools of Martial Arts

　　中国武术门派众多，往往依托山川名胜自然形成，诸如少林、武当、峨嵋、崆峒、天山、昆仑、华山等各派武术，都是依托佛教、道教名山，形成闻名中外的武术流派。

There is a great variety of sects and schools in Chinese martial arts which are usually named after the mountains and geographical landmarks where they were born. For example, such schools of martial arts which enjoy fame at home and abroad like *Shaolin, Wudang, Emei, Kongtong, Tianshan , Kunlun, Huashan* and the like were all formed on famous Buddhist and Taoist mountains.

> 少林武术

少林武术是中国武术之宗，是中国武术中范围最广、历史最长、拳种最多的武术门派，在武术文化中占有举足轻重的地位，正所谓"天下武术出少林，少林武术甲天下"。

河南登封的嵩山少林寺是少林武术的发祥地。北魏时期（386—534），天竺僧人跋陀来到中国，受到孝文帝的礼敬，太和十九年（495），孝文帝命人在嵩山建寺供养跋陀。北魏孝文帝太和年间（477—499），印度南天竺禅宗第二十八代祖师菩提达摩来到少林寺传授佛教禅宗，被尊为中国佛教禅宗的初祖，少林寺也因此被誉为"中国佛教禅宗祖庭"。

武以寺名，寺因武显。少林寺

> *Shaolin* Martial Arts

As the mainstream of Chinese martial arts, *Shaolin* Martial Arts has the broadest scope, the longest history, and the largest variety of fist techniques. It occupies a decisive position in the culture of Chinese Martial Arts. Well goes the saying that "All martial arts come out of *Shaolin*; *Shaolin* Martial Arts exceeds in the world."

The *Shaolin* Temple of Mount Song in Dengfeng of central China's Henan Province is the birth place of *Shaolin* Martial Arts. During the Northern Wei Dynasty (386-534), an Indian monk, Batuo, came to China and was reverently received by Emperor Xiaowen. In the nineteenth year of Taihe (495), Emperor Xiaowen ordered a temple to be constructed in Mount Song as an offering to Batuo. During the Taihe years (477-499) under the reign of the Emperor

● 嵩山少林寺（图片提供：全景正片）
The *Shaolin* Temple in Mount Song

之所以名传古今，主要是因为发展了少林武术的缘故。关于少林武术的创立，民间有多种传说。相传，达摩终日面对石壁，静坐冥思，不免筋骨疲倦，便仿效劳动人民锻炼身体的动作，糅合了鸟兽虫鱼的姿势，编成健身养性的动作，成为少林拳的雏形。还有一种传说，少林武术源于第一代祖师跋陀的弟子慧光和僧稠，这两位弟子身体健壮，身怀绝技，精通武术，他们将武术带入了少林寺。

Xiaowen in the Northern Wei Dynasty, Bodhidharma, the twenty-eighth Patriarch of the Buddhist sect of *Chan* (also known as Zen Buddhism), came from South India to visit the *Shaolin* Temple and teach Zen Buddhism. He was revered as the first Patriarch of Chinese *Chan* sect, and the *Shaolin* Temple was therewith honored as the "Ancestral Temple of Chinese *Zen* Buddhism".

The martial arts are named after the temple, while the temple is noted for its martial arts. The fame of the

• 《达摩面壁图》【局部】宋旭(明)
Bodhidharma Facing the Wall [Partial]
by Song Xu (Ming Dynasty, 1368-1644)

以上两个传说，并没有史籍可考。实际上，北朝时的寺院有练武的风气，少林武术是少林寺僧众在长期参禅、修道、护寺和健身的实践中创立的。少林武术吸纳了中国武术流派的精华，把中国武术与禅宗相融合，经过不断发展完善，形成了讲究实用、内容丰富、风格独特的武术门派，以刚劲威猛、禅武合一、博大精深的武术之风饮誉天下，又有"武术禅"之称。

Shaolin Temple has been passed on from the past to the present mainly because of the *Shaolin* Martial Arts it has developed. There are a variety of legends with regards to the origin of *Shaolin* Martial Arts. According to the legend, Bodhidharma was sitting in meditation all day long against the stone wall. In order to soothe inevitable fatigue and cramping, he followed the exercise movements of the working people and blended in with the postures of animals, birds, insects and fish, which were subsequently compiled into moves to strengthen the body and cultivate nature. They became the prototype of *Shaolin Quan* (fist). Another legend has it that *Shaolin* Martial Arts originated from Batuo's two disciples, Huiguang and Sengchou. They were physically strong and capable of special feats with mastery in martial arts. It was these two disciples who brought martial arts to the *Shaolin* Temple.

These two above-mentioned legends have no historical records for reference. In fact, the climate of practicing martial arts had already been around in temples during the Northern Dynasties (386-581). *Shaolin* Martial Arts was created out of the *Shaolin* monks' long-term practice of *Chan (Zen)* meditation,

練習少林武術的僧人 (圖片提供: FOTOE)
Monks Practicing *Shaolin* Martial Arts

隋唐时期，少林武术已具盛名，少林寺从僧众当中选出身强力壮者进行武术训练，让他们担当护卫寺院的任务。后来，少林寺寺僧还参与了政治活动，寺养僧兵。在有关少林寺的故事当中，以十三棍僧助唐王最富传奇色彩。

少林寺声名远播，各地的武林高手、英雄豪杰纷纷慕名而来，以武会友，切磋武艺，促进了少林

monasticism, temple protective measures and fitness exercises. It had absorbed the essence of different sects of martial arts in China and integrated Chinese Martial Arts with *Chan (Zen)* Buddhism. Through continuous development and improvement, a rich-in-content, practicality-oriented and unique-styled martial arts school was formed. With its strong, powerful and fast style, *Chan-Wushu* integrated cultivation, as well as extensive and profound nature, it has

十三棍僧助唐王

公元7世纪初，唐王李渊、秦王李世民父子在讨伐王世充的作战中，少林寺13位武艺高强的僧人协助李渊父子，奋力作战，迫使王世充投降。李世民登基后，对少林武僧大加封赏，并赐少林寺良田，扩充庙宇，建立僧兵，僧众达5000多人。从此，少林寺名声大振，进入兴盛时期，被誉为"天下第一名刹"，僧众论武、习武之风盛行。

Thirteen Staff Warrior Monks Helped the King of Tang

In the early 7th century, when the King of Tang, Li Yuan, and his son, Li Shimin (King of Qin Area) were engaged in a crusade war against Wang Shichong, they were helped by 13 monks from the *Shaolin* Temple with extraordinary feats of martial arts, whose devoted fight eventually forced Wang Shichong to surrender. After Li Shimin ascended to the throne and became the Emperor, he profusely rewarded the *Shaolin* monks and bestowed fertile land to the *Shaolin* Temple. The Temple was also augmented and allowed to establish monk troops, which totaled more than 5,000 people. Since then, the *Shaolin* Temple rose to great fame and was hailed as "the First Famous Temple of the World" as it entered into its prosperity period. The fashion for monks to discuss and practice martial arts became prevalent.

武术的发展。相传，宋代的开国皇帝赵匡胤是少林寺的俗家弟子，曾得过少林真传。赵匡胤喜爱练武习艺，创编了多种套路。金元时期少林寺的觉远大师曾邀请武林高手李叟、白玉峰等到少林寺传授武功、切磋武技，一起研讨拳术、剑术、棍术、擒拿等功夫。觉远大师为少林武术的发展作出了巨大的贡献，

gathered itself a reputation and renown from all over the world. It is also known as *Wushu Chan* (Zen of Martial Arts).

By the Sui and Tang Dynasties (581-907), *Shaolin* Martial Arts had already enjoyed great prestige. In the temple, strong and powerful monks were selected to undergo training for *Shaolin* Martial Arts and assume the task of guarding the monasteries. Later in

少林寺壁画
Mural Painting of *ShaoLin* Temple

time, *Shaolin* monks were also involved in political activities, and the temple began to train monk soldiers. The most legendary tale among the stories of the *Shaolin* Temple was the one about how the thirteen staff warrior monks came to the aid of the King of Tang.

The reputation of the *Shaolin* Temple was so widely spread that many heroes from different places were attracted by its fame to study martial arts together and befriend each other, which further promoted the development of *Shaolin* Martial Arts. According to legend, the founding Emperor of the Northern Song Dynasty (960-1127), Zhao Kuangyin, was a lay disciple of the *Shaolin* Temple who had obtained the true heritage of *Shaolin* Martial Arts. Zhao Kuangyin enjoyed practicing martial arts and fist fighting skills. He had never composed a variety of *Tao Lu* or forms. During the Jin and Yuan Dynasties (1115-1368), Master Jueyuan of the *Shaolin* Temple once invited martial arts master Li Sou and Bai Yufeng to teach martial arts and exchange views at the *Shaolin* Temple. They studied and discussed various *Gong Fu*, such as fist fighting, swordsmanship, staff techniques, *Qin Na* (catching tactics) and so on. Master

被后世尊为少林拳法的"中兴之祖"。少林寺经常邀请各地武林高手到寺里传授武艺，明代抗倭名将俞大猷就曾到少林寺传授棍术。

● 俞大猷像
Statue of Yu Dayou

Jueyuan made significant contributions to the development of *Shaolin* Martial Arts and was later regarded as the Revival Patriarch of *Shaolin* fist fighting techniques. The *Shaolin* Temple often invited martial arts masters from different places to come and teach martial arts at the Temple. Yu Dayou, a famous general that fought against *Wo Kou* (Japanese pirates) during the Ming Dynasty, was teaching the staff techniques at the *Shaolin* Temple.

Shaolin Martial Arts worked with other schools and made mutual improvements by learning from each other's strong points to offset the weakness. Over time, it gradually developed into a martial arts school composed of fist fighting forms, *San Da* (free-style fighting), weapon forms and exercise techniques. Being extensive and profound, *Shaolin* Martial Arts is not only rich in content, but also teeming with sophisticated forms. According to the records of training manuals passed down within the Temple, *Shaolin* currently has 708 forms of martial arts, including 552 sets of fist fighting and weapon forms. Beyond that, there are a total of 156 categorized drill works such as the 72 unique feats, *Qin Na*, *Qi Gong* (inner-

● 名震世界的少林武术 (图片提供：全景正片)
World-famous *Shaolin* Martial Arts

少林武术与诸家流派取长补短，互相促进，日积月累，逐步发展成为由拳术套路、散打、器械、功法等组成的武术流派。少林武术博大精深，内容丰富，套路繁多，据少林寺内传的拳谱记载：少林武术套路现存708套，其中拳术和器械套路为552套，另外七十二绝技、擒拿、气功、格斗、点穴、卸骨等各类功法有156套。

energy techniques), *Ge Dou* (grappling techniques), *Dian Xue* (acupoint hitting) and *Xie Gu* (bone-dislocating techniques).

> 武当武术

在中国武术界，有"南尊武当，北崇少林"之说，可见武当武术与少林武术在中华武术文化中的地位和影响。武当武术汲取中国传统养生的精髓，集武术技击之大成，把古代太极、阴阳、八卦、五行等哲学理论用于练功原则和技击方法中，以松沉自然、外柔内刚的独特风格自成体系。

武当山雄踞于湖北省西北部丹江口市西南，奇峰竞秀，风景秀丽。武当山是道教真武大帝的道场，保留着中国规模最大的道教宫观建筑群。

人们谈起武当武术的历史，首先想到元末明初的武当全真道士张三丰，认为他是武当武术的开山祖师。张三丰受阴阳平衡、八卦演

> *Wudang* Martial Arts

In the world of Chinese martial arts, there is a saying that "*Wudang* is respected in the south, and *Shaolin* is revered in the north". It manifests the status and influence that *Wudang* Martial Arts and *Shaolin* Martial Arts have enjoyed the culture of Chinese martial arts. *Wudang* Martial Arts has drawn the essence of Chinese traditional life-nourishing ideas, and accumulated the great achievements of fighting skills. It applies the philosophical theories of *Tai Chi*, *Ying and Yang*, *Ba Gua* (the Eight Diagrams) and *Wu Xing* (the Five Elements) in the principles of its practice and fighting skills, featuring the unique styles of total relaxation and natural gravitation (*Song Chen Zi Ran*), as well as being soft on the outside and tough in the inside (*Wai Rou Nei Gang*) as its distinguished system.

The *Wudang* Mountains reside in

太极

太极一词出自《易经》，
"太"是大的意思，"极"则代表
极端，是最初的意思。所谓"太
极"，意思是达到了极限，没有相
匹之意，也包含了至大、至小的时
空极限的道理。中国古代思想家认
为太极代表了宇宙的起源，是天地
混沌、阴阳未分之前的原始状态，
并把太极视为产生世界万物的本
原，代表了天地万物产生、演变的
过程。

Tai Chi

The term *Tai Chi* originates from *The Book of Changes*. "*Tai*" means large, and "*Ji*" means extremity. The so-called "*Tai Chi*" means that the extreme limit has been reached, where there is no match. It also includes the concept of the extremely greatest and smallest limitations of space and time. Ancient Chinese thinkers believed that *Tai Chi* represented the origination of the universe in a state where the heaven and the earth were still in chaotic unity and *Yin* and *Yang* were undifferentiated. *Tai Chi* is viewed as the very source where all things in the world originated. It represented the creation of the heaven and the earth, and the process of evolution.

阴阳

中国古代思想家观察到一切
现象都有正反两方面，如天地、日
月、昼夜、寒暑、男女等，因此归
纳出"阴阳"的概念来解释自然界
两种对立和相互消长的现象。阴阳
学说认为事物普遍存在"阴"、
"阳"两种相互对立的属性，阴阳
相反相成是事物发生、发展、变化
的规律和根源。

Yin and Yang

Ancient Chinese thinkers observed that all phenomena had both a positive and a negative aspect, such as the heaven and the earth, the sun and the moon, day and night, summer and winter, male and female, and so forth. Therefore, they utilized the concept of *Yin* and *Yang* to explain the phenomena of mutual opposition, and mutual waning and waxing in nature. The *Yin* and *Yang* theory holds the idea that the prevalent attributes of *Yin* and *Yang* in mutual opposition underlie everything in the world. The mutual opposition and mutual complement between *Yin* and *Yang* are the law as well as the root of all things in their origination, development and change.

武术的著名门派

Famous Sects and Schools of Martial Arts

五行

中国古代思想家认为世界万物都是由金、木、水、火、土五种物质构成的，这五种物质之间存在着既相互促进又相互制约的关系，得出"五行相生相克"的理论。金生水、水生木、木生火、火生土、土生金，叫做"五行相生"；金克木、木克土、土克水、水克火、火克金，叫做"五行相克"。

The Five Elements

Ancient Chinese thinkers believed that all things in the world are composed of the five elements of metal (gold), wood, water, fire and earth (soil). These five elements exist in a relationship of mutual generation and restriction, a theory called "the mutual generation and elimination of *Wu Xing*". Gold generates water, water generates wood, wood generates fire, fire generates soil, and soil generates gold. This is known as the *Wu Xing Xiang Sheng* (inter-promotion of the five elements). On the other hand, gold destroys wood, wood destroys soil, soil destroys water, water destroys fire and fire destroys gold. This is called the *Wu Xing Xiang Ke* (inter-restriction of the five elements).

八卦

八卦是用阳爻（——）和阴爻（— —）组成的八种基本图形，每卦由三爻组成。八卦的名称是：乾、坤、震、巽、坎、离、艮、兑，象征天、地、雷、风、水、火、山、泽八种自然现象，每卦又象征多种事物。"乾"、"坤"两卦在八卦中占有非常重要的地位，是自然界和人类社会一切现象的最初根源。

Ba Gua

Ba Gua comprises eight diagrams based on the *Yang Yao* (——) and the *Yin Yao* (— —). Each diagram is a trigram composed of three *Yaos*. The names of the eight *Gua* are: *Qian, Kun, Zhen, Xun, Kan, Li, Gen* and *Dui*, which respectively signify the eight natural phenomena of heaven, earth, thunder, wind, water, fire, mountain, and lake. Each *Gua* is a symbol of multiple things. The diagrams of *Qian* and *Kun* play very important roles in *Ba Gua*. They are the root source of all phenomena in the natural world as well as the human society.

武术
Chinese Martial Arts

变、五行生克等思想的影响，把道家的内丹功法、养生家的导引术、各派武术的拳法加以糅合，创编出适合防身自卫、保健养生的武当内家拳。

the southwest of Danjiangkou City in the northwestern region of Hubei Province, with grotesque peaks and beautiful scenery. The *Wudang* Mountains host the temple site of Zhenwu Dadi (Great Emperor of True Martial Arts), which still retains the largest group of

- 武当山

  武当山是道家文化发源地，也是武当武术的发祥地。

  The *Wudang* Mountains

  The *Wudang* Mountains are the birthplace of Taoist culture, and also the birthplace of *Wudang* Martial Arts.

中国武术史上的张三丰

张三丰在中国武术史上是一个充满神秘色彩的人物，历史上同名同姓的张三丰还不止一人。后人常常把一些拳术的编创之功归至张三丰。因此关于张三丰创编拳法的传说也很多。一个是宋代的武当山道士张三丰，武艺高强，据说曾受宋徽宗召见。他在赴京城的途中，梦到神人传授武艺，创出内家拳。另一个是元末明初的武当山道士张三丰，精通少林拳，在云游时无意中看到鹰蛇相斗，得到灵感，创出武当内家拳。

Zhang Sanfeng in the History of Chinese Martial Arts

Zhang Sanfeng is a mysterious figure in the history of Chinese Martial Arts. There was more than one person in history that shared the name of Zhang Sanfeng. In later generations, people used to title the compilation or creation of their own fist fighting techniques as of Zhang Sanfeng. As a result, many legends exist with regards to Zhang Sanfeng's invention of martial arts techniques. One of them is about the Taoist Zhang Sanfeng on the *Wudang* Mountains with outstanding prowess in martial arts during the Song Dynasty. He was said to have once been summoned by Emperor Huizong of the Song Dynasty. On his way to the capital, he dreamed that a man of God imparted martial art techniques onto him, which he later utilized to create the *Nei Jia Quan*. Another Taoist from the *Wudang* Mountains also went by the name of Zhang Sanfeng in the late Yuan Dynasty and early Ming Dynasty, who was proficient in *Shaolin Quan*. He was inspired by a scene of an eagle fighting against a snake while he was traveling, and later created the internal style of *Wudang Nei Jia Quan*.

张三丰像
Portrait of Zhang Sanfeng

内丹功法

内丹功法是道教重要的炼养方术之一，是以天人合一思想为指导，以人体为鼎炉，以体内的精、气为药物，以神烧炼，在体内凝练结丹的修行方式。

Nei Dan Technique

The *Nei Dan* (internal alchemy) technique is one of the important cultivation techniques of Taoism. As a cultivation practice, it takes the concept of man and heaven integration as a form of guidance, using the human body like a furnace, *Jing* (essence) and *Qi* (inner energy) in the body as medicinal materials, and *Shen* (soul) as the cooking fire in order to form a condensed "*Dan*" (pellet, or ball) within the body.

其实，武当武术的渊源要追溯到很久以前，早在张三丰之前，武当武术就已经有了漫长的历史。据《太和山志》、《均州志》记载，自周朝以来，就有道士和炼丹家在武当山的深山岩洞之中，弃绝世俗，静心养性。武当山的道士过着

architectures of Taoist temples in China.

When people speak of the history of *Wudang* Martial Arts, the first thing that comes to their mind is the Quanzheng-sect Taoist, Zhang Sanfeng, from the *Wudang* Mountains in the late Yuan Dynasty and early Ming Dynasty, presumably the founding patriarch of *Wudang* Martial Arts. Zhang Sanfeng was influenced by such ideas as *Yin-Yang* balance, *Ba Gua* evolution and the mutual generation and elimination of *Wu Xing*. He combined the internal alchemy (*Nei Dan*) of Taoism with *Dao Yin* (guiding) techniques of regimen masters as well as those martial arts techniques from various sects and created the *Nei Jia Quan* (internal style) of *Wudang* Martial Arts, suitable for self-defense, self-protection as well as health care and preservation.

In fact, the origin of *Wudang* Martial Arts can be traced far way back in history. *Wudang* Martial Arts had already had a long history prior to Zhang Sanfeng. In the records of *Taihe Mountain History* and *Junzhou History*, Taoists and Alchemists were already present in the caves of the remote *Wudang* Mountains in the Zhou Dynasty (1046 B.C.-256 B.C.), practicing

导引术

　　导引是中国古代一种强身健体的养生方法，是按照一定规律和方法，以主动的肢体运动，配合呼吸吐纳或自我按摩而进行的锻炼。通过适当运动，达到防病保健、延年益寿的目的，相当于现代的体育疗法。

Dao Yin Technique

Dao Yin is a healthcare method for physical fitness in ancient China. It is a form of workout that utilizes proactive limb movements, coupled with respiratory breathing and self-massage in accordance with certain rules and methods. Through proper exercises, it can achieve the goals of disease-proof health and longevity. It is equivalent to the physical therapy of modern times.

● 《导引图》摹本

　　《导引图》是现存最早的一卷保健运动的工笔彩色帛画，1974年在湖南长沙马王堆三号汉墓出土。《导引图》共有44幅小型全身导引图，从上到下分四层排列，每层各有11幅小图。

A Copy of the *Chart of Dao Yin*

The *Chart of Dao Yin* is currently the earliest color brushwork on silk containing health exercises. It was unearthed in 1974 from the third Tomb of Han in Mawangdui of Changsha city of central China's Hunan province. The *Chart of Dao Yin* contains a total of 44 small-sized, full-body illustrations, arranged in four rows from top to bottom, each of which contains 11 small pictures.

● 表演武术的武当山道徒 (图片提供：FOTOE)
Martial Arts Performance by *Wudang* Taoists

与世无争的生活，讲究清静无为，探求养生之道，很早就有练拳的传统，其练拳的主要目的在于养气健身、制敌自卫。

经过历代宗师的继承发展，武当武术派生出众多门派和种类，成为体系庞大、独树一帜的武术流派。流传至今的武当派拳路不下六十种，包括太极拳、形意拳、八卦拳、太乙五行拳、太和拳等。

武当派的器械套路也有几十种，如太极枪、武当剑、玄武棍、

cultivation and meditation in seclusion from the secular world. These Taoists in the *Wudang* Mountains led an aloof life free from the conflicting of the world. They emphasized *Qing Jing* (quietism) and *Wu Wei* (non-action) and studied regiment. Although they had already had a long tradition of practicing martial arts, the main purpose of their martial arts training was mainly to maintain health through *Qi* cultivation and to defense themselves against enemies.

After successive development by grand masters through generations, *Wudang* Martial Arts has branched out a multitude of various sects and categories and become a school of martial arts with a gigantic system and unique features of its own. There have been no less than 60 different *Wudang* fist fighting styles that have been passed down up to now, including *Tai Chi Quan, Xing Yi Quan, Ba Gua Quan, Taiyi Wu Xing Quan, Taihe Quan,* and so on.

There are also dozens of different types of *Wudang* weapon techniques, including *Tai Chi* spear, *Wudang* swordplay, *Xuanwu* staff, *Sanhe Dao* (*Sanhe* blade), *Fangbian Chan* (convenient shovel), and *Fu Chen* (horsetail whisk) among others. *Wudang*

三合刀、方便铲、浮尘等。武当拳派中还包含若干功法，比较著名的有活气功（类似"铁布衫"功）、和血功（重在养生）、打穴功等。

武当武术的功法特点是强健筋骨，注重内功修炼，以养生为首，防身为要，动作讲究以柔克刚、以静制动、以慢击快，舒缓沉稳、柔和自然、圆融贯通，主张借力打力、四两拨千斤、后发制人的打法，追求清静无为、随心所欲的境界。

Martial Arts also comprises a number of special exercise techniques, including the famous *Huo Qi Gong* (similar to *Tie Bu Shan*, or iron cloak), and *Xue Gong* (blood skills, focused on health), and acupoint hitting skills.

The characteristic of the exercise work of *Wudang* Martial Arts is in the strengthening of bones and muscles with stress on internal cultivation. The primary concern is health, followed by self-defense. Its moves pay particular attention to using softness to curtail toughness, inaction to restrict action, and slow moves to attack fast moves. They are soothing, calm, soft, natural and harmonious. These movements aim to leverage the power of others as their own, and strikes only after skillful deflecting an attack. They aim to pursue tranquility, inaction, and free flow at will.

● 练剑的武当派弟子 (图片提供：FOTOE)
Wudang Disciples Practicing Sword

> 峨眉武术

峨眉武术与少林武术、武当武术同样有着悠久的历史，共为中原武功的三大流派，尤其是在中国西南地区独占鳌头。

峨眉武术之所以得名，是因发源地峨眉山而起。峨眉山位于中国四川省中南部，与浙江普陀山、安徽九华山、山西五台山并称为"佛教四大名山"。峨眉武术深受道教、佛教的宗教文化，以及四川独特的民风、民俗等地域文化影响，融各派武术之长，经过长期发展，成为独具特色的武术流派。

关于峨眉武术的起源，民间传说纷繁复杂，为峨眉武术增添了不少神秘色彩。例如，相传东汉时期的火龙真人撰写了《参同契》，峨眉山道士根据书中理论，模仿猿猴

> *Emei* Martial Arts

Like *Shaolin* and *Wudang*, *Emei* Martial Arts also has enjoyed a long history. Together, they are the three major schools of martial arts in the Central Plains, especially in the southwest region of China.

Emei Martial Arts is so called because it originated from the *Emei* Mountain. Located in the central and southern region of China's Sichuan Province, the *Emei* Mountain along with *Putuo* Mountain in Zhejiang, *Jiuhua* Mountain in Anhui, and *Wutai* Mountain in Shanxi are known as the Four Famous Mountains of Buddhism. *Emei* Martial Arts is deeply influenced by the religious cultures of Taoism and Buddhism, as well as the regional cultures of the unique folk customs and styles of Sichuan. *Emei* Martial Arts has become a unique school of martial arts after a long term

动作创编了火龙拳。在中国武侠小说大师金庸所著的《倚天屠龙记》中，记载了郭襄创立门派的说法：

of development with strong points of various sects blended in.

A number of complicated folklores regarding the origination of *Emei* Martial Arts have added a shroud of mystery to *Emei* martial arts. For example, legend has it that Huolong Zhenren (the immortal one of fire dragon) of the Eastern Han Dynasty (25-220) composed *Can Tong Qi*, and in accordance with the theory in the book, the Taoists of *Emei* created *Huo Long Quan* (the Fire Dragon Fist) in imitation of the actions of apes. In the novel *The Heaven Sword and Dragon Saber* by Jin Yong, a master writer of Chinese *Wu Xia* tales, the school was said to be founded by Guo Xiang as follows: Guo Xiang was the daughter of Guo Jing, a hero from Xiangyang, and Huang Rong in the Southern Song Dynasty (1127-1279). She was traveling

云雾缭绕中的峨眉山 （图片提供：全景正片）
Emei Mountain Shrouded in Mist

Wannian Temple in *Emei* Mountain

郭襄是南宋时期襄阳大侠郭靖和黄蓉的女儿，她云游天下，后大彻大悟出家为尼，创立峨眉派。这种说法因《倚天屠龙记》的大量发行而广为传播，但实际上，这只是小说的创作而已。比较流行的说法是，相传春秋战国时期的司徒玄空耕食于峨眉山中。他模仿猿猴动作，在狩猎术的基础上创编了一套通臂拳。因为司徒玄空常穿白衣，徒众们便称他为"白猿祖师"。

魏晋时期，道教和佛教传入峨眉山，受宗教文化影响，武术得到了发展。道士、高僧们汲取了道教的养生之道和佛教的禅修，发展完

the world when her sudden enlightenment changed her into a nun and the founder of the School of *Emei*. This explanation of the origination of *Emei* Martial Arts prevailed because of the wide distribution of *The Heaven Sword and Dragon Saber*. In actuality, this story is but fiction from the novel. A more popular legend tells that during the Spring and Autumn and Warring Periods (770 B.C. – 221 B.C.), a man named Situ Xuankong was plowing the land for something living in *Emei* Mountain. By imitating the actions of apes, he created a set of techniques called *Tong Bi Quan* based upon hunting skills. Since Situ Xuankong often wore a white robe, his followers called him the "White Ape Patriarch".

During the Wei and Jin Dynasties, Taoism and Buddhism were introduced to *Emei* Mountain. Influenced by the religious culture, *Emei* Martial Arts achieved progress and development. Taoists and monks absorbed Taoist regimen and Buddhist Zen cultivation to develop a perfect sect of martial arts that integrated toughness with softness, combined the static with the dynamic and coupled the internal techniques with the external ones.

After the Song Dynasty (960-1279),

• 峨眉武术 "白猿祖师" 塑像 (图片提供：FOTOE)
The Statue of White Ape Patriarch

善了刚柔相济、动静结合、内外兼修的武功。

宋代以后，峨眉山作为普贤菩萨的道场，成为中国佛教名山。峨眉山香火旺盛，僧人甚多，其中习武者不少。南宋建炎年间（1127–1130），峨眉山金顶寺高僧白云禅师根据道家内养炼丹术、导引吐纳法和人体盛衰之机理，与武术中的动静功法、技击之术相融

Emei Mountain became a famous Chinese Buddhist mountain as the temple site for Samantabhadra Bodhisattva. The *Emei* Mountain thrived in burnt incense and housed a great number of monks, many of whom were martial artists. During the reign of Jianyan in the Southern Song Dynasty (1127-1130), Zen Master Baiyun of the *Jinding* Temple in *Emei* Mountain based his study on the Taoist internal alchemy, *Dao Yin* and breathing techniques, and the mechanism of waning and waxing in human body, coupled with the static and dynamic exercises and fighting skills in martial arts, and created *Emei Qi Zhuang Gong*, also known as the Twelve *Zhuang Gong* of *Emei*. During the Southern Song Dynasty, another monk from *Emei* Mountain, Deyuan the Elder, imitated the climbing and jumping movements of apes, and created the Ape Fist. Since Deyuan the Elder had white eyebrows, Ape Fist also came to be known as the *Bai Mei Quan* (white eyebrows fist) in the martial arts world. In Deyuan the Elder's Quan Shu, a systematic summary was provided for *Emei* Martial Arts, which became a self-contained hallmark of the matured development of *Emei* Martial Arts.

Emei Martial Arts saw an

● 峨眉枪 (图片提供: FOTOE)
Emei Spear

合，创编出峨眉气桩功，又称"峨眉十二桩功"。南宋时期，另一位峨眉山僧人德源长老，模仿猿猴攀爬腾跃的动作，创编了一套猿拳。因为德源长老眉毛纯白，所以武术界又将猿拳称为"白眉拳"。德源长老著有《拳术》，书中对峨眉武术做了系统总结，成为峨眉派武术发展成熟并自成体系的标志。

明清时期，峨眉武术得到空前的发展。在明代唐顺之的《荆川先生文集》里，有一首《峨眉道人拳歌》，生动形象地描述了峨眉道人的深厚武术功夫。峨眉派的枪法、

unprecedented development during the Ming and Qing Dynasties (1368-1911). In the Ming Dynasty, Tang Shunzhi's *Collected Works of Mr. Jing Chuan* contained a "Fist Song of the *Emei* Taoist", which vividly described the profound martial arts techniques of the *Emei* Taoists. The *Emei*-style spear techniques, swordplay and others among the Eighteen Arms of Martial Arts techniques had also reached the highest point of proficiency. In the Ming Dynasty, Wu Shu's *Shou Bi Lu* chronicled the protean techniques of *Emei* spear and included such subjects as mind cultivation, body cultivation, quietism-orientation, dynamism-orientation, offense and defense, examination of situations, alert and scrutiny, backhand, jabbing techniques, and counter-weapon moves among others, which enriched the theories of *Emei* Martial Arts. In the Qing Dynasty, as *Emei* Martial Arts was widely circulated, so many subdivisions and sectors emerged that over 300 of them were known as unique schools and sects, such as the Monkey Fist, Ox Horn Fist, the Fire Dragon Fist and Duck Fist.

Emei Martial Arts have complicated and overloaded contents. Its fist fighting techniques, weapons skills and practice methods have not only absorbed the

剑法等十八般兵器的技法，也达到了炉火纯青的地步。明代吴殳的《手臂录》一书，记叙了变幻莫测的峨眉枪法，内容有治心、治身、宜静、宜动、攻守、审势、戒谨、倒手、扎法、破诸械等，丰富了峨眉武术的理论。清代，峨眉拳术广为流传，形成了很多派别，独具特色的有三百多种，如猴拳、牛角拳、火龙拳、鸭形拳等。

峨眉武术内容繁杂，拳术、器械及练功方法既汲取了少林、武当等各派的精华，又独具特色。峨眉派武术讲究内外兼修，形神合一，刚柔并济，开合有度。少林、武当、峨眉三派相比较，少林派阳刚，以攻架见长，多用长手；武当派阴柔，以呼吸见长，多用短手；峨眉派亦柔亦刚，内外相重，长短并用，攻防兼具。

峨眉武术主张动静并重，有著名的"动功十二桩"——天、地、之、心、龙、鹤、风、云、大、小、幽、冥；又有"静功六大专修功"——虎步功、重捶功、缩地功、悬囊功、指穴功、涅槃功。峨眉武术出手指掌当先，身法柔活，

essence of various schools like *Shaolin*, *Wudang*, and others, but also established its unique features. The *Emei* School of martial arts stresses the integrated internal and external cultivation, the unity of body with mind, the combined usage of toughness and softness, and the self-controlled degree of opening up and closing up. When compared, the *Shaolin* school is masculine, specialized in offense, and characterized by long-range usage of hand techniques; the *Wudang* school is feminine, specialized in breathing techniques, and characterized largely by short-range usage of hand techniques; and the *Emei* school is characterized by the combined manifestations of both the tough style and the soft style, the internal and external techniques, the long-range and short-range exercises as well as the offensive and defensive approach.

Emei Martial Arts advocates the combined usage of both the static and dynamic movements. In the dynamic part, there are the famous Twelve *Zhuang* of Dynamic Techniques: *Tian* (sky), *Di* (earth), *Zhi* (going), *Xin* (heart), *Long* (dragon), *He* (crane), *Feng* (wind), *Yun* (cloud), *Da* (large), *Xiao* (small), *You* (tranquil), and *Ming* (darkness); For

● 1953年全国民族形式体育表演竞赛大会
上表演峨眉刺的马喜善 (图片提供：FOTOE)
Ma Xishan Performing the *Emei* Pierce
at the National Forms and Sports
Performance Competition in 1953

善用五峰六肘之力，五峰即头、
肩、肘、臀、膝；六肘指上肘、下
肘、左肘、右肘、回肘、倒肘。

峨眉武术有"三大器械"——
剑法、簪法（峨眉刺）、针法（暗
器）。峨眉派的剑法和簪法，姿势优
美，但威力十足，是峨眉的绝技。

the static, there are the Six Specialized Techniques of Static Techniques: *Hu Bu Gong* (the Tiger Step Technique), *Zhong Chui Gong* (the Heavy Hammer Technique), *Suo Di Gong* (the Land Shrinking Technique), *Xuan Nang Gong* (the Sack Lifting Technique), *Zhi Xue Gong* (the Pressure Point Technique), and *Nie Pan Gong* (the Nirvana Technique). In *Emei* Martial Arts, attacks are delivered by outstretched fingers and the palm in the front. The body moves in soft but agile ways in order to make the best use of the power of the five peaks and the six elbows. The five peaks are the head, shoulder, elbow, hip and knee. The six elbows refer to the upper elbow, the lower elbow, the left elbow, the right elbow, the back elbow, and the reverse elbow.

Emei Martial Arts also have the techniques of Three Main Weapons—the sword, the hairpin (*Emei* pierce), and the needle (hidden weapon). *Emei's* swordplay and hairpin techniques utilize beautiful postures but are filled with power. Together, they both are the unique techniques of *Emei* Martial Arts.

> 崆峒武术

崆峒山是崆峒派武术的发源地，位于甘肃省平凉市西，是中国历史上的道家名山。

崆峒武术是道家俗家武术门派，起源较早，中国第一部辞书《尔雅》中记载："崆峒人武。"据传崆峒武术由唐代道人飞虹子所创。崆峒武术将武术与道家思想融会结合，以技击、强身健体为目的，在技击手法、套路上自成一体。

崆峒武术共分八大门类，分别是飞龙门、追魂门、夺命门、醉门、神拳门、花架门、奇兵门和玄空门。每门各有十余套拳术和器械套路。崆峒武术的动作以柔美为主，身法、步法、手法多以弧线、曲线形成，具有美感。所用器械短

> *Kongtong* Martial Arts

Kongtong Mountain in the west of Pingliang City of north China's Gansu Province is the birthplace of *Kongtong* Martial Arts. It has been a famous mountain of Taoism in Chinese history.

Kongtong Martial Arts is a branch of the Taoist school for lay disciples. It showed up at a very early age. The first book of lexicon in China, *Er Ya*, records that: "People of practice martial arts." According to legend, *Kongtong* Martial Arts was created by a Taoist in the Tang Dynasty (618-907) named Fei Hongzi. It combines martial arts with Taoist thinking, sets fighting skills and physical fitness as its main purpose, and asserts its own style in the handwork of fist fighting and forms.

Kongtong Martial Arts is divided into eight major sub-categories, namely the *Feilong Men* (Flying Dragon School),

● 崆峒山风光

崆峒山奇险灵秀，集自然景观和人文景观于一身，自古就有"西来第一山"、"崆峒山色天下秀"之美誉。

Scenery of *Kongtong* Mountain

Kongtong Mountain is delicate, yet uniquel and dangerousl, beautiful. It embodies both the natural and the cultural landscape, and has long held the reputation of "The NO.1 mountain in the West" and "the great scenery of *Kongtong* Mountain being renowned across the world."

小、轻柔、奇特，如扇、拂尘、鞭等。这些奇门兵器是崆峒武术的一大特点，不属于十八般兵器，形式多样，小巧轻便，便于携带，在交手中往往能出奇制胜。

Zhuihun Men (the Soul Chaser School), *Duoming Men* (the Life Snatching School), *Zui Men* (the Drunken School), *Shenquan Men* (the Holy Fist School), *Huajia Men* (the Floral Rack School), *Qibing Men* (the Grotesque Martial School), and *Xuankong Men* (the

峒崆武术 (图片提供：FOTOE)
Kongtong Martial Arts

Profound Void School). Each school has more than a dozen forms of fist fighting techniques and weapon skills. The movements of *Kongtong* Martial Arts are featured by a soft sense of beauty. Its body movements, footwork and hand techniques are delivered in arc lines and curves with an aesthetic touch. All of the weapons used are small and short, soft and light, and somewhat strange, such as fans, dusters, and whips. These unique weapons are one of the major characteristics of *Kongtong* Martial Arts. Though they are outside of the category of the Eighteen Arms of Chinese Martial Arts, they are various in form—compact, lightweight and easy to carry. In actual fights, they are often able to execute surprise attacks.

> 天山武术

天山山系呈东西走向，横贯中国新疆维吾尔自治区中部，西端伸入哈萨克斯坦和吉尔吉斯斯坦。天山派武术始创于南宋光宗绍熙元年（1190年），至今已有八百多年的历史。天山派武术的祖师杨继明是

• 天山风光 (图片提供：全景正片)
Scenery of *Tianshan*

> *Tianshan* Martial Arts

The *Tianshan* Mountain system extends from the east to the west over the west of China and parts of Kazakhstan and Kyrgyz. It is one of the largest mountain ranges in Asia. *Tianshan* Martial Arts was founded in the first year of Shaoxi (1190) under the reign of Emperor Guangzong in the Southern Song Dynasty (1127-1279). It has enjoyed 800 years of history up to now. The founder of *Tianshan* Martial Arts, Yang Jiming, was a descendant of renowned general, Yang Jiye, in the Northern Song Dynasty (960-1127). In his childhood, he practiced the martial arts of the *Dan Ding* (Red Furnace) School under the tutor of Wang Shiguang, the ninth generation descendant of the Taoist Master Ge Hong in the Jin Dynasty. As the Southern Song Dynasty declined and chaotic wars occurred, he retreated into seclusion in the Western Regions (around the Bogda Mountain region in *Tianshan*

北宋名将杨继业之后，他幼年时师从晋代葛洪真人的第九代传人王世光，习练丹鼎派武术，后因南宋衰落，战事纷乱，远遁西域（今新疆天山山脉博格达山区）隐居，习练武功，修道养性。

杨继明之子杨延天与当时同隐天山的道教神霄派王文卿之徒萨守坚，结伴同修，一起创派并制规。天山派第三代传人张志平将天山派功法融合了全真教之修真教义，完善了天山派的功法和派规。

天山派功法是以道门丹鼎派内功为基础，并融会了神霄派心法和杨氏家传武功，从而形成了自己独特的体系，讲究内练心神，外练身形，以外补内，玄人天一，求得修仙达真的境界。因天山派武术属于隐修派，历经沧桑，其不少拳种后世罕有所闻。

Mountain of the current Xinjiang) to practice martial arts and monastic cultivation.

At the time, Yang Jiming's son, Yang Yantian, worked in self-cultivation with Sa Shoujian, a disciple of the Taoist of Shenxiao Sect, Wang Wenqing, and created the school and formulated its regulations. The third-generation descendant of the *Tianshan* School, Zhang Zhiping, blended in the martial arts of the *Tianshan* School with the cultivation doctrine of Quanzhen Taoism and enhanced the martial arts skills and regulations of the *Tianshan* Sect.

The Martial Arts of *Tianshan* School were based upon the internal cultivation of the *Dan Ding* School and combined the mental practice of the Shenxiao Sect with the hereditary martial arts of the Yang family to form its own unique system. It emphasizes the internal training of the mind, external training of the body and the use of external exercise to complement the internal exercise. It aims at the unity of the profound truth, human, and heaven, and the search for the state of immortality to attain the truth. Due to the hermitic nature of the school as well as the vicissitudes it has experienced, fewer fist fighting styles of *Tianshan* Martial Arts had been heard of by later generations.

> 昆仑武术

昆仑派武术继承中华武术的传统，在拳术、器械、对练等方面有独特的创造。其技法奇特，内容丰富，既有技击护身之功，又有健身益年之术。

昆仑派武术源于昆仑山地区，

• 昆仑山
Kunlun Mountains

> *Kunlun* Martial Arts

Kunlun Martial Arts has inherited the traditions of Chinese Martial Arts, and created its own uniqueness in terms of fist fighting techniques, weapon skills and *Dui Lian* (paired-up fighting drills). Its extraordinary techniques and rich content can provide not only the skills of defense but also benefits of health and fitness.

The School of *Kunlun* Martial Arts originated from the region of the *Kunlun* Mountains, located in the eastern part of the Pamirs Plateau. The wavy mountain range with its tranquil environment has been praised in the Chinese Taoist culture as "the ancestor of all mountains". The School of *Kunlun* Martial Arts later spread along with immigrants to the neighborhood of Henan province and has had a history for over 200 years.

The *Kunlun* fist fighting technique is the hallmark of *Kunlun* Martial Arts. It is

昆仑山地处帕米尔高原东部，山脉连绵起伏，环境清幽，在中国道教文化里，有"万山之祖"之誉。后来昆仑派武术随移民传至河南一带，至今已有二百多年历史。

昆仑拳是昆仑武术的代表。昆仑拳矫健有力，动作迅速快猛。手型多变，攻防结合，手脚并用，步法灵活、扎实。

昆仑派长期秘传的气功——大雁功，是模仿大雁形态，结合气功导引法编成的一套高级功法，其功效能舒筋活血，防治疾病，保健强身。

a vigorous and strong fighting style with fast and fierce movements. Its variety of hand styles, offensive and defensive combinations, and integrated exercise of hands and feet are complemented with flexible and solid footwork.

Kunlun School's time-honored esoteric *Qi Gong, the Dayan Gong*, is a kind of exercise which imitates the form of wild geese and incorporates *Dao Yin* methods to form a set of advanced techniques. This technique can function to register effective medicinal properties, prevent diseases and maintain physical health.

异彩纷呈的拳术
A Kaleidoscope of Fist Fighting Techniques

　　武术是一种传统体育项目，经过数千年的发展，形成了众多拳术流派。这些拳术流派技法各异，风格各有千秋，极大地丰富了武术的内容。按拳种的风格特点划分，有内家、外家两大类；按地域划分，有南派、北派之说。流传至今的拳术有一百多种，以下是对主要的拳种作些介绍。

Martial arts are traditional sport, which have branched out a variety of fist fighting techniques after thousands of years of development. These fist fighting techniques of different schools and sects are so different in styles and strong points, but they have greatly enriched the contents of martial arts. Fist fighting techniques have been classified in relation to their unique characteristics in two main categories: the internal style and the external style. Geographically classified, there are the Southern style and the Northern style. The sets of fist fighting techniques handed down till today boast over 100 varieties, and below are the introductions to some major sects.

> 少林拳

少林拳得名于河南嵩山少林寺，这是在中国古代健身术的基础上，集各种武艺之长而形成的，在国内外均享有盛名，有"天下功夫出少林"的美誉。

少林寺僧众传习拳术、发愤习武的记载最初见于《旧唐书·稠禅师传》。经过历代研练和总结，少林拳融汇了众家拳法之长，逐步发展成为内容丰富、体系完整的拳术，留传后世。

少林拳注重实用，套路结构紧凑，动作朴实，刚健雄武，快猛疾速，攻防严密，招式多变，力量运用得灵活而有弹性。"拳打一条线"是少林拳的一个鲜明特点，出拳滚动而发，起落进退常直来直往。

少林拳要求在技击时身进步相

> *Shaolin Quan (Shaolin Fist Fighting)*

Shaolin Quan is named after the *Shaolin* Temple in Mount Song, Henan Province. It is based on ancient Chinese fitness techniques and has gathered the strong points of various martial arts. Renowned both at home and abroad, *Shaolin* Martial Arts hold the reputation that "All martial arts originated from *Shaolin*."

The determined effort of *Shaolin* monks in learning and teaching martial arts can be found in the original tale of *The Biography of Zen Master Chou* in *Old Book of the Tang*. After being studied, practiced and summarized through so many generations, *Shaolin Quan* has converged the best techniques of various schools, and gradually developed into a complete and content-rich system of martial arts, passed on from generation to generation.

Shaolin Quan stresses practicality,

● 习武的少林僧人
Shaolin Monk Practicing Martial Arts

with compact structures in forms, simplicity in moves, masculine toughness in actions, and quickness and fierceness in agility. It has a tightly connected network of offense and defense, a repertoire of changeable forms and a flexible way of using power. A distinctive feature of the *Shaolin Quan* lies in the motto that "punches should follow a straight line." Rolls of punches are delivered and advances and retreats are made all along straight lines.

Shaolin Quan demands that in fighting, when the body moves forward, the steps should be brought along and the heart is to regulate the breath, or *Qi*, before an action is taken. The stress is laid on that an attack should be "elegant like a cat, vibrant like a tiger, maneuverable like a dragon, fast like a bolt of lightning, and loud like roars of thunder." The body has to rise unexpectedly, fall smoothly, and move flexibly. There are eight key points in moves: *Qi* (rise), *Luo* (fall), *Jin* (advance), *Tui* (retreat), *Fan* (return), *Ce* (sideway move), *Shou* (restrain), and

随，心动气先行，有"秀如猫、抖如虎、行如龙、动如电、声如雷"的讲究。身法起横落顺，灵活多变，有起、落、进、退、反、侧、收、纵八个动作要点。步法低进高退，轻灵稳固。站桩功是少林拳的基本功，桩有马步桩、椅子桩、丁字桩等，同时也练视、听、抓、

● 少林拳对练 (图片提供: FOTOE)
Paired-up Sparring Drills of *Shaolin Quan*

拉、推、举、踢等。

少林拳的内容庞杂，有拳法套路、器械等。拳术有单练和对练两种，单练有小洪拳、大洪拳、罗汉拳、炮拳、长拳、梅花拳等套路，对练有六合拳等。少林拳除了徒手拳术，还有刀、枪、剑、棍等十八般兵器的器械操练。

Zong (release). Footwork should be low in advance and high in retreat, agile but yet firm. The *Zhan Zhuang Gong* (Static Stance) is a basis of *Shaolin Quan*. The stance includes the Horse Stance, the Chair Stance, and the "T" Stance. At the same time, the practice of sight, hearing, grasping, pulling, pushing, lifting and kicking among others is also demanded.

The rich contents of *Shaolin Quan* include various fist fighting forms and weapon techniques among others. There are two kinds of fist fighting disciplines, *Dan Lian* (single-man drills) and *Dui*

站桩功

站桩功是中国武术特有的一项训练，是武术内功的基本功法，有"要学拳，须站桩；欲习打，先练桩"的说法。"桩"是比喻身体如木桩一样站立不动，坚实稳固。武术的桩功种类很多，各门各派武术多有自己的桩功。桩功以站式为主，身体保持特定的姿势，使全身或某些部位的松紧度呈持续的静力性运动状态。除了静态的形式外，还有在走动中练习的行桩，又称"动桩"。

Zhan Zhuang Gong (the Static Stance)

As a unique aspect of Chinese martial arts training, *Zhan Zhuang Gong* (the Static Stance) is a basic technique of the internal style of martial arts. As the saying goes, "To learn how to fight, one must start with *Zhuang*; to learn how to punch, one must first practice *Zhuang*." *Zhuang* (literally, a stake) is a metaphor for the body standing fixed and firm like a wood stake. There are various types of *Zhuang* in martial arts and different schools or sects have their own different *Zhuang*. The Static Stance is based upon the standing posture while the body is maintained in a specific posture. It can hold the entire body or a certain part of the body in a sustained static state with a certain degree of tightness in force. In addition to the static form, there are also stances that are practiced during movement, known as the *Dong Zhuang* (Dynamic Stances).

Lian (paired-up fighting drills). The single-man forms include the *Xiao Hong Quan* (small *Hong* Fist Fighting), *Da Hong Quan* (big *Hong* Fist Fighting), *Luo Han Quan*, *Pao Quan* (Cannon Fist Fighting), *Chang Quan* (Long Fist Fighting) and *Mei Hua Quan* (Plum Flower Fist Fighting) among others. The paired-up sparring includes *Liuhe Quan* (Six-direction Fist Fighting) and others. There are also *San Da* (free style) and *Qi Gong* (breathing exercise). Aside from bare-hand martial arts, *Shaolin Quan* also has the techniques of the 18 Arms of Martial Arts, such as the blade, spear, sword, staff and others.

> 内家拳

内家拳是武当派的代表功夫。武当拳的特点是重视内功的修炼，强调意识引导动作，讲求后发制人，以静制动，以柔克刚，以逸待劳，乘势借力。因其主于防守，有别于以攻为主，注重锻炼拳脚功夫，交手时主张先发制人，刚硬直击的外家拳（少林拳），故称"内家拳"。

融养生于技击之中，这与偏重技击的佛门拳派少林拳有所不同，武术界一般将武当拳称为"内家拳"，将少林拳称为"外家拳"。

关于内家拳的源流，据明末清初的学者黄宗羲（1610—1695）所作的《王征南墓志铭》记载，内家拳是由武当道士张三丰始创的。《内家拳法》一书中也说，张三丰

> *Nei Jia Quan* (Internal Style)

Nei Jia Quan is the representative martial art of the *Wudang* School. The unique feature of *Wudang Quan* is its emphasis on the cultivation of internal strength. It stresses such characteristics as actions guided by consciousness, posterior strategies, use of inaction to conquer action, use of softness to overcome toughness, use of relaxation to wear out the opponent's labor, and the use of the opponent's power against themselves. Its defensive strategy distinguished itself in stark contrast to those schools and sects of the external style that are based primarily on offense, with stress placed on the well-trained punches and kicks in their tough-oriented and straightforward strategy of preemptive moves and offensive measures (as in *Shaolin Quan*). It is henceforth called *Nei Jia Quan*.

● 习练内家拳的武当山道士 (图片提供：FOTOE)
Taoists Practicing *Nei Jia Quan* in the *Wudang* Mountains

精通少林拳，经过对少林拳的改造，创编出内家拳。

内家拳是少林武术与内功结合的产物，是将"外练筋骨皮"与"内练精气神"融为一体，并对少林拳进行了改造。它以道教的理论为指导，结合中医、易学、养生学等知识，把技击与强身健体并举。

内家拳在技击上有自己的特点，主张后发制人，以静制动，拳法多变，多用掌而少用拳，不像少林拳多是出拳直击。内家拳法较少

By blending regimen cultivation into fighting techniques in direct contrast to the Buddhist *Shaolin* School, *Wudang Quan* makes itself drastically different so that *Wudang Quan* is called the "*Nei Jia Quan*" while *Shaolin Quan* is called the *Wai Jia Quan* (external style).

According to the recorded Epitaph for Wang Zhengnan by Huang Zongxi (1610-1695), a scholar in the late Ming and early Qing Dynasties, *Nei Jia Quan* was founded by the *Wudang* Taoist, Zhang Sanfeng. The book *Nei Jia*

• 张三丰雕像
Statue of Zhang Sanfeng

跳跃动作，步型低，重在擒拿。

内家拳讲求"点穴法"，在与对方交手时，有意识地点击对手经络上的一些特殊穴位，这些穴位被称为"麻穴"、"哑穴"、"晕穴"、"死穴"，麻、哑、晕、死各九穴，习惯上说是三十六穴。这些穴位若用手指、肘、膝、脚等迅猛点击，可以使气血的运行受阻，造成生理机能的暂时失调，会出现疼痛、酸软、昏迷甚至死亡的现

Quan Techniques also states that Zhang Sanfeng, who was skilled in the *Shaolin Quan*, modified *Shaolin Quan* and created the *Nei Jia Quan*.

Nei Jia Quan is the product of the combination of *Shaolin* Martial Arts and *Nei Gong* (internal techniques). It unites the "external training on muscle, bone and skin" with the "internal training of *Jing* (essence), *Qi* (inner energy) and *Shen* (soul, or mental power)", and makes modifications on *Shaolin Quan* so as to create its internal style. With Taoist theory as its guidance, *Nei Jia Quan* integrates the knowledge of traditional Chinese medicine, the study of *the Book of Changes* and the regimen of life force preservation, making fighting techniques and physical fitness into one.

Nei Jia Quan also has its own characteristics in its posterior strategies, with utilization of inaction against action, changeful fist fighting techniques and frequent use of the palm instead of the fist. This sets it apart from *Shaolin Quan*, which generally uses fist punches. *Nei Jia Quan* contains fewer jumping moves, low stances and is more focused on *Qin Na* (catching tactics).

Nei Jia Quan emphasizes *Dian Xue Fa* (acupoint-hitting method). When

象。内家拳高手们都有相当高超的点穴技术，但是穴有生穴、死穴之分，这关系到人的生死存亡，不能轻易传授给他人。加之点穴法不易掌握，所以古代武术家们对点穴法只采取口授的方法。

据《内家拳法》记载，内家拳

engaged in the fight with the opponent, the practitioner will intentionally pinpoint his attack onto some specific acupuncture points on the opponent's body. These acupuncture points are known as *Ma Xue* (numbness points), *Ya Xue* (mute points), *Yun Xue* (unconsciousness points), and *Si Xue* (death points). Each of them has nine acupuncture points. Therefore, they are usually referred to as the thirty-six acu-points. When these points are forcefully hit by a finger, elbow, knee, foot and so on, the circulation of blood and *Qi* will be blocked so that temporary disorientation of physiological functions in the form of pain, limpness, unconsciousness and even death may be caused as a result. *Nei Jia Quan* masters usually have superb acu-point striking skills. Since acu-points involve the difference between points of life and points of death, a matter of life and death, the teaching of these techniques is not to be taken lightly. Moreover, due to its difficulty to be mastered, the techniques of acu-point

拳师表演内家拳 (图片提供：FOTOE)
Fist Fighting Master Performing *Nei Jia Quan*

经络与穴位

中国古代中医理论认为，经络（经脉和络脉的统称）是人体气血流通的通道，像一张大网把全身上下、内外联结在一起。穴位又称"腧穴"，是人体脏腑经络之气输注于体表的部位，从头顶到脚跟，全身共有三百多处穴位。点穴法就是根据中医经络学说的理论设计的。

Meridians and Acupuncture Points

The ancient Chinese medicine theory held the idea that *Jing Luo* (*Jing Mai,* meridian channels, and *Luo Mai*, collateral channels, collectively known as "meridians") are the passages within the human body that *Qi* and blood flow through. Like a massive network, *Jing Luo* spread across the entire human body, linking together the upper part and lower part of our bodies, as well as the interior and exterior of the human body. *Xue Wei* (acupuncture points, also known as "acupoints") are the loci where the *Qi* in the meridians of internal organs flow to the exterior surface of the human body. From head to heel, there are more than 300 acupoints all over the human body. The martial art of acupoint attacks is based on the meridian theory of traditional Chinese medicine.

• **针灸铜人**

针灸铜人是中国古代针灸教学的人体模型，始创于宋天圣四年（1026年）。用铜塑造成一个青年男子形象，体表刻有经络和腧穴名称，身体内有脏器。

Bronze Acupuncture Figure

The bronze acupuncture figure is a pedagogic model of the human body used in ancient Chinese acupuncture education. It was first made in the fourth year of Tiansheng in the Song Dynasty (1026). The bronze figure was cast in an image of a young man with meridian lines and names of acupoints marked on the surface, and organs inside of the figure.

除了强调内功修炼和点穴法外，还有35种手法、18种步法、72种跌法等。

明清时期，内家拳一开始主要在武当山和浙江东部一带流传，后传至四川、江苏等地。至今武当山的道士们仍然保持着练内家拳的传统。

attack have been transmitted via oral instruction by the martial artists since ancient times.

According to the descriptions in *Book of Nei Jia Quan Techniques*, *Nei Jia Quan* also includes 35 kinds of hand techniques, 18 kinds of footwork, and 72 take-down techniques along with the emphasized practice of internal cultivation and acupoint techniques.

During the Ming and Qing Dynasties (1368-1911), *Nei Jia Quan* began to circulate in the *Wudang* Mountains and east of Zhejiang Province. It later spread to Sichuan, Jiangsu and other places. Today, the Taoists in the *Wudang* Mountains still maintain the traditional practice of *Nei Jia Quan*.

> 太极拳

　　在中国武术中，最能体现中国人性格气质的莫过于太极拳。太极拳合技击与养生为一体，是一种意气运动。它要求以心行气、以气运身，意动形动，意到气到，气到劲到，劲由内换，柔中有刚，刚柔相济。太极拳像行云流水，绵柔不断，有人称它"绵拳"，这种拳术由八种手法和五种步法构成，也有人称它"十三势"。清乾隆年间（1736—1795）王宗岳所写的《太极拳论》，以太极理论阐述太极拳的拳理，使太极拳的名称固定下来。"太极"一词，最早出自战国时期的哲学著作《周易》中，指天地未分时的混沌元气，《周易》认为世上万物都是由这种元气变化产生的。太极拳沿用了太极理论，既

> *Tai Chi Quan (Tai Chi* Fist Fighting)

Among all the Chinese Martial Arts, *Tai Chi Quan* best embodies the temperament and character of Chinese people. *Tai Chi Quan* is an exercise of mind and *Qi* that combines fist fighting techniques with regimen cultivation. It requires the use of the mind to regulate the flow of *Qi* and the use of *Qi* to move the body. When the mind moves, the body moves; when the mind reaches to a point, the *Qi* reaches along; when *Qi* reaches a point, the power reaches it too. Since the power generated is converted from the inner energy, toughness resides in softness and the softness and toughness complement each other. The movements of *Tai Chi Quan* are like the flowing of clouds and a running river. They are softly flowing without interruptions. That's why *Tai Chi Quan* is also called *Mian Quan*

表示这种拳以元气为基础，又说明这种拳充满无穷的变化，却万变不离其宗。

在技击原则上，太极拳坚持重在防御，以守为攻，以退为进。太极拳高手们一般不主动进攻，而是防范周严，后发制人；多是等待对方进攻，一搭上手，即粘住不放，舍己从人，顺对方进击的方向，以

(Unbroken Fist). Since it is composed of eight hand moves and five footwork moves, people also call it "the Thirteen Moves". During the reign of Qianlong in the Qing Dynasty (1736-1795), the book *On Tai Chi Quan,* written by Wang Zongyue, expounded the *Tai Chi* theory applied in the rationale of *Tai Chi Quan*, and thereupon settled the official name of *Tai Chi Quan*. The term "*Tai Chi*" first appeared in the philosophical work of *Zhou Yi* (*Book of Changes*) during the Warring States Period (475 B.C.-221 B.C.). It signifies the original *Qi*, or *Yuan Qi*, in the great chaos where the Heaven and the Earth were undifferentiated. *The Book of Changes* proposes that all things on Earth were produced from this original *Qi*. Since *Tai Chi Quan* follows the theory of *Tai Chi*, it means that *Tai Chi Quan* is based upon the original *Qi*. It further implicates that *Quan* is full of inexhaustible changes while all changes are not disrupted from the original state.

The principle of fighting in *Tai Chi Quan* insists upon defense—using defense as a form of offense and using retreat as a form of advance. In general, *Tai Chi Quan* masters won't initiate an attack, but hold on to tight defense instead for the purpose of posterior strategies. In essence, they wait for the opponent's attack and once they can attach the hand onto the opponent, they will not lose contact. Their body will then follow the

异彩纷呈的拳术

A Kaleidoscope of Fist Fighting Techniques

● 太极拳练习者
Practitioner of *Tai Chi Quan*

● 左手缠丝

缠丝是太极拳一个非常特别的行拳特点，行拳时掌心的运动内外翻转，呈螺旋状，表现出了太极图的圆形和"S"形曲线。上下、左右缠丝是一个太极圆；里外结合，从平面到立体又形成了太极球。

Left-hand *Chan Si*

Chan Si (entangled silk thread) is a very special characteristic of the *Tai Chi Quan*. When delivering the move, the palms of the hands flip from inward to outward or vice versa through a spiral movement in imitation of the circular shape and the "S" curves in the *Tai Chi* diagram. Moving from the top to the bottom and from the left to the right, a circle of *Tai Chi* is formed in *Chan Si*. To progress it further from the inside to the outside, the two-dimensional *Tai Chi* diagram will change into a three-dimensional *Tai Chi* ball.

弧形动作化开对方的劲力，借力打力，发挥"四两拨千斤"的特长。

太极拳由一系列螺旋缠绕动作组成，每个动作都呈圆形。从外观上看，太极拳全部是划圆的动作，与其他拳派迥异。在行拳时，太极拳利用离心力原理，以腰为轴，节节贯穿，以内气催动外形，示柔缓于外，寓刚疾于内。行拳者的一切动作皆为内圈，而始终置对方于外圈。这样，即便内圈的动作慢些，仍可胜过外圈的"快"，易使对方

direction of the opponent's attacks and make curving movements to neutralize the opponent's attack or leverage the opponent's power against himself in order to fulfill the special feat of *Tai Chi Quan*—"releasing grams to leverage tons".

Tai Chi Quan is composed of a series of entangled spiral movements. Every action takes on a circular form. In appearance, all the moves in *Tai Chi Quan* are delivered in circular movements, making it quite different from other schools of martial arts. When executing an attack, *Tai Chi Quan* applies

失去重心。行拳者在舒缓潇洒的旋转之中，随时可以骤然发劲。太极拳的发力多是弹抖之劲，称为"寸劲"。这是在极短距离内，于刹那间爆发出来的一种合力，其劲甚短，其发极速，其力冷脆，具有较大的威力。不少人以为太极拳动作迟缓，无法用于技击，其实是一种误解。

• 北京北海公园里太极拳练习者
太极拳以其健身、防病、抗衰老的养生功效，成为一项全民健身运动。
Practitioners of *Tai Chi Quan* at Beihai Park in Beijing
Tai Chi Quan has become a nationwide fitness sports thanks to its benefits of physical fitness, disease prevention and anti-aging effects.

the principle of centrifugal force and uses the waist as an axis to spin out pushing force. While the inner *Qi* motivates the external form, softness and slowness will be shown in appearance while solid and tough force is being formed inside. All the moves will enclose oneself in the inner ring, and the opponent will be kept in the outer ring. This way, even a slow movement of the inner ring is able to out-speed the fast movement of the outer ring and spin the opponent out of balance. In the ostensible, slow and relaxed moves of a *Tai Chi* practitioner, a sudden burst of power can be made at anytime. The force exerted in *Tai Chi Quan* is usually generated from abrupt snapping power, known as "*Cun Jin*" (inch power). It is a short abrupt burst of synthesized power, executed in an instant with great speed, solid force and tremendous effects. Many people believe that the slow movements of *Tai Chi* cannot be utilized in combat. However, it is actually a misconception.

Tai Chi Quan emphasizes the use of inaction against action, softness against toughness, weakness against strength, slowness against speed, less against more and skillfulness against awkwardness. It's taboo for a *Tai Chi* practitioner to use awkward force in blind, undisciplined moves, or apply

太极拳讲究以静制动，以柔克刚，以弱胜强，以慢胜快，以少胜多，以巧胜拙，最忌以拙力死拼滥打、硬顶硬抗。太极拳是一种蕴含着深奥哲理、充满了智慧的拳术，集中体现了中国人对人生、对宇宙的悟解，以及中国人的处世之道，是中国传统文化的一种特殊表现形态。

如今太极拳作为一项健身项目，已风靡世界，传播到五大洲１５０多个国家和地区。长期习练太极拳有助于锻炼身体和思维，减轻压力，延缓衰老，使人重获生机和活力，美国《时代》杂志称其为"完美运动"。

tough power against tough power. *Tai Chi Quan* is a special kind of martial arts which contains a profound philosophical idea and deep wisdom. It condenses and embodies the Chinese people's comprehension of life and the universe, as well as their way of communication. It is a special manifestation of the traditional Chinese culture.

As a specific item of fitness sports, *Tai Chi Quan* has been popular nowadays throughout the world, and has spread over 150 countries and regions across the five continents. A sustained practice of *Tai Chi Quan* helps to exercise the body and mind, reduces stress, delays aging and revitalizes people's life and energy. The U.S. Times magazine called it "the perfect exercise".

太极拳的起源和流派

关于太极拳的起源，武术界一直存在着争论。多数意见认为太极拳起源于河南焦作温县陈家沟，为陈王廷（1600—1680）所创。陈王廷为明末清初人，原学家传武功。清军入关以后，他曾在登封玉带山参加反清武装斗争，事败后回归故里，隐居三十年，潜心研究武学，终于创编出独具一格的太极拳。

The Origin and Schools of *Tai Chi Quan*

Controversy still exists in the world of martial arts regarding the origin of *Tai Chi Quan*. The majority of people hold the opinion that it originated from a place called Chenjiagou of

Wen County, located in Jiaozuo of central China's Henan Province, and was created by Chen Wangting (1600-1680) of the late Ming and early Qing Dynasties. Chen Wangting originally practiced family-inherited martial arts. After the Qing army entered the Shanghai Pass, he used to participate in an armed anti-Qing uprising in Yudai Mountain, located in Dengfeng. After returning home in defeat, he went into seclusion for thirty years to concentrate on his studies of martial arts, and finally completed the unique style of the *Tai Chi Quan*.

陈王廷之后，太极拳一直在陈氏族人中传授，人称"陈式太极拳"。直到晚清时期，太极拳才开始外传，以北京为中心，衍化出杨（杨式太极拳）、武（武式太极拳）、孙（孙式太极拳）、吴（吴式太极拳）四大流派。

After Chen Wangting, *Tai Chi Quan* continued to be taught in Chen's clan and was known as the *Chen*-style *Tai Chi Quan*. It wasn't until the late Qing Dynasty when *Tai Chi Quan* began to spread outside of the clan. With Beijing as the center, it gradually evolved into the four main schools of *Tai Chi Quan*: *Yang* (Yang-style *Tai Chi Quan*), Wǔ (Wǔ-style *Tai Chi Quan*), Sun (*Sun*-style *Tai Chi Quan*), and Wú (Wú-style *Tai Chi Quan*).

　　杨式太极拳始于杨福魁（1799—1872）。他是河北永年人，早年家贫，被温县陈家沟某陈姓大户购为僮仆，在陈家沟遇陈式第十四代陈长兴，学艺十余年，拳艺初成。杨福魁后来在北京屡挫名手，人称"杨无敌"，被推荐到王府授拳。当时，在王府学拳的多是王公贵族子弟，体质娇嫩，杨福魁便将陈式太极拳中一些难度较大的动作做了修改，使之不纵不跳，趋于简单柔和，又经其子孙修改，成为"杨式太极拳"。

Yang-style *Tai Chi Quan* began with Yang Fukui (1799-1872). Originally from Yongnian County of north China's Hebei Province, he was born in a poor family and was purchased in his early years by a wealthy Chen family from Chenjiagou of Wen County to serve as a child servant. In Chenjiagou, he met Chen Changxing, the fourteenth generation descendant of the *Chen*-style *Tai Chi Quan*, and spent more than a decade learning the Chen style until he could fully master the techniques. With his acquired martial arts skills, Yang Fukui defeated a lot of famous martial artists in Beijing, and was thus known as the Invincible Yang. He was subsequently recommended into royal families to teach martial arts. At that time, children of the noble families learning martial arts were mostly of delicate physique. Yang Fukui then modified some of the difficult moves from the *Chen*-style *Tai Chi Quan*, eliminated jumps and leaps, and made it simpler and gentler. With further modifications made by his descendants, the current version of "Yang-style *Tai Chi Quan*" was thus established.

武式太极拳

Wǔ-style Tai Chi Quan

　　武式太极拳始于武禹襄（1812—1880）。他也是河北永年人。杨福魁从陈家沟艺成回永年后，武禹襄便从他学拳。随后，武禹襄又拜陈式第十五代陈青萍为师，学习陈式小架（太极拳的拳架依动作幅度的大小，可以分为大架、小架，拳架动作幅度大的称作"大架"，拳架动作幅度小的称作"小架"）。其后，武禹襄把杨式大架和陈式小架结合起来，形成了"武式太极拳"。

The *Wǔ*-style *Tai Chi Quan* began with *Wǔ* Yuxiang (1812-1880) from Yongnian County of Hebei Province. When Yang Fukui returned to Yongnian from Chenjiagou, *Wǔ* Yuxiang began learning techniques from him. Later on, *Wǔ* Yuxiang sought apprenticeship again from the fifteenth generation descendant of the *Chen*-style *Tai Chi Quan*, Master Chen Qingping, and learned the *Xiao Jia* (small frame) of the *Chen*-style techniques. The physical structure performed in *Tai Chi Quan* can be divided into *Da Jia* (big frame) and *Xiao Jia* (small frame) according to the size of their range of motion. The fist style with a larger range of motion is known as the *Da Jia*, and the style with a smaller range of motion is known as the *Xiao Jia*. Later, *Wǔ* Yuxiang combined the *Da Jia* of the Yang style with the *Xiao Jia* of the Chen style and created the *Wǔ*-style *Tai Chi Quan*.

孙式太极拳始于孙禄堂（1861—1932）。孙禄堂是河北完县人，早年为形意拳、八卦掌名家，在北京有"活猴"之称。他在50岁那年，拜武禹襄的再传弟子郝为真为师，融形意、八卦、太极为一体，创编了架高步活、开合鼓荡的"孙式太极拳"。

Sun-style *Tai Chi Quan* started with Sun Lutang (1861-1932) from Wan County of Hebei Province. Sun Lutang was originally a master of *Xing Yi Quan* and *Ba Gua Zhang* in his early years, and was nicknamed Live Monkey in Beijing. At the age of 50, he was apprenticed to Hao Weizhen, a disciple of *Wǔ* Yuxiang, and combined the *Xing Yi, Ba Gua* and *Tai Chi* together in his *Sun*-style *Tai Chi Quan* featured by a high stance, agile footwork and broad opening and closing.

吴式太极拳始于吴鉴泉（1870-1942）。吴鉴泉是北京人，满族，后改汉姓为吴。他的父亲曾先后师从杨福魁父子学拳。后来，吴鉴泉在杨式父子拳架基础上，加以改进修润，使之更趋于柔和，形成了"吴式太极拳"。

The Wú-style *Tai Chi Quan* began with Wú Jianquan (1870-1942). Originally from Beijing, Wú Jianquan was a Manchurian, but he changed his name to the Han surname Wú. His father learned the fist techniques successively from Yang Fukui and his son. Based on the techniques of Yang Fukui and his son, Wú Jianquan modified the technique and made it gentler and softer. That's the Wú-style *Tai Chi Quan*.

　　到了民国初年，由陈式太极拳衍化而出的杨、武、孙、吴各成一派，闻名久远的太极拳系才算真正形成。太极拳在中国诸大拳系中形成最晚，但它是最富于活力的一支。

In the early years of the Republic of China (1912-1949), when the lineages of Yang, Wǔ, Sun, and Wú branched out and established their own styles, the whole system of the long-famous *Tai Chi Quan* was truly formed. Although *Tai Chi Quan* was the last to be formed among all the major systems of Chinese fist fighting techniques, it is the most active one indeed.

八种手法图解
Eight Hand Techniques

- 按
  双手按住对方身体
  发力的部位。

  An (Push):
  Push down the
  opponent on the part
  delivering force.

- 将
  化劲，根据对方的来劲，进行力
  的分解或转化。

  Lu (Roll Back):
  Dissolve or transform the force
  coming from the opponent.

- 采
  用手以柔劲抓、拿、掏，粘带对方
  用来进攻的相应部位，将其制住。

  Cai (Pluck or Grasp):
  Use the hand to grasp, seize, pull out
  or adhere to the attacking part of the
  opponent in a flexible way, aiming to
  bring the opponent under control.

- 肘
  以肘击人。

  Zhou (Elbow
  or Elbow
  Strike):
  Strike with the
  elbow.

- 掤

遇敌时以坚韧的纯刚之劲将对方击退或使对方不能靠近。

Peng (Ward Off):

Beat back or make the opponent unable to approach by using force with pure hardness.

- 挤

用手或肩、背挤住对方使其不得动。

Ji (Press):

Make the opponent unable to move by pressing with the hand or the shoulder and back.

- 挒

用向外横推之力，使对方身体扭转而失重。

Lie (Split):

Push outward horizontally to force the opponent to turn the body and thus lose balance.

- 靠

用肩、背向外击人。

Kao (Shoulder or Shoulder Strike):

Strike with the shoulder or back.

五种步法图解
Five Steps

定
原地不动，不发力，做好准备。
Ding (Central Balance):
Stand motionless, use no strength and make preparation.

盼
注视对方的眼神，由对方的眼神来判断其动作方向。
Pan (Right Step):
Stare at the opponent's eyes and tell in what direction the opponent will move.

进
在对方被制住或重心不稳时，及时向前踏进或发力。
Jin (Forward Step):
Step forward or strike when the opponent is controlled or out of balance.

顾
避开对方的正面而由两旁绕进，以避实就虚。
Gu (Left Step):
Approach the opponent from one side, rather than straight forward, to attack an area not guarded.

退
包括防御和进攻，防御用于引进落空，进攻用在边退边攻，退中求打。
Tui (Backward Step):
Used for both defense to lead the attacker into emptiness, and attack while retreating.

> 形意拳

形意拳与太极拳、八卦掌齐名，是一种模仿动物形象的拳术。它不仅模仿动物活动的形象，学习动物的进攻技巧，还模仿动物动作的内意，由心产生意，又由意转化为拳，又称"心意拳"。

形意拳由山西蒲州（今山西永济县）人姬际可（1602—1680）所创。姬际可精通武艺，曾在少林寺习武十年，汲取了少林拳、武当拳等拳法特点，创编了心意拳。在心意拳的传人中，河北深县人李飞羽（约1808–1890）认真总结前人经验，结合自己多年练拳经验，把"心意拳"改名为"形意拳"，形意拳的理论体系逐渐形成。

清代，形意拳在山西、河北、河南等地广泛流传，形成了不同风格的各种流派，如山西流传的形意

> *Xing Yi Quan* (Fist of Intention)

Just as famous as the *Tai Chi Quan* and *Ba Gua Zhang*, *Xing Yi Quan* is a fist fighting technique that imitates the forms of animals. Not only does it copy the appearance of animal movements and incorporate the attacking skills of animals, but also mimic the inner mindset of the animal movements, using the mindset to generate the intent, and transforming this intent into a fighting move. Hence, it is also known as the *Xin Yi Quan* (Fist of Intention).

Xing Yi Quan was created by Ji Jike (1602-1680) from Puzhou of Shanxi (current Yongji county of Shanxi Province). Ji Jike was skillful in martial arts. He studied martial arts for 10 years in *Shaolin* Temple, and extracted the characteristics from various schools like *Shaolin* and *Wudang* to

拳，拳势紧凑，劲力精巧；河北流行的形意拳，拳势舒展，稳健扎实；河南一带的形意拳，拳势勇猛，气势雄厚。近百年来，形意拳名手辈出，威震武林。

形意拳以六合为法，练习此

● 形意拳
形意拳的动作严密紧凑，发拳时，拧裹钻翻，动作刚而不僵，柔而不软。
Xing Yi Quan
The movements of *Xing Yi Quan* are tightly connected and compact in sequence. When a punch is delivered, it might twist, wrap, drill and then turn. All the moves are solid rather than stiff, and are soft but not weak.

create the *Xin Yi Quan*. Among the successors of *Xin Yi Quan*, Li Feiyu (ca. 1808-1890) from Shen county of Heibei Province conscientiously summed up the experiences of those before him, combined them with his many years of martial arts experience, and renamed *Xin Yi Quan* as *Xing Yi Quan*. The theoretical system of *Xing Yi Quan* was thus formed gradually.

In the Qing Dynasty (1644-1911), *Xing Yi Quan* was so widely practiced in places like Shanxi, Hebei, Henan, and others that various derivative styles were formed as a result. For example, the kind of *Xing Yi Quan* practiced in Shanxi has its moves delivered in a compact, impulsive yet delicate way; on the other hand, the kind of *Xing Yi Quan* from Hebei is stretched, steady and solid in form; still, the *Xing Yi Quan* practiced in the vicinity of Henan is strong and fierce in an imposing way. In the last century, *Xing Yi Quan* has given birth to a large number of skillful martial artists and resonated within the martial art community.

Xing Yi Quan utilizes *Liu He* (Six Harmonies) as its laws. To practice this fist technique, the *Nei San He* (Inner Three Harmonies) and the *Wai San He*

拳有"内三合"、"外三合"的
要求。内三合指心与意合，意与气
合，气与力合，即身体内部几种因
素紧密结合；外三合指肩与胯合，
肘与膝合，手与足合，即行拳时肢
体各部分的协调配合。所以形意拳
又称"心意六合拳"。

- 形意拳
形意拳动作简洁朴实，动作大多直来直
往，一屈一伸，节奏鲜明，富有自然之
美。

Xing Yi Quan

The movements of *Xing Yi Quan* are simple
and plain. Its actions are generally delivered
in a straight line, punctuated with bends and
stretches with distinct rhythm, teeming with
natural beauty.

(Outer Three Harmonies) are required.
The *Nei San He* refers to the harmonies of
the mind with the intent, the intent with
the *Qi,* and *Qi* with *Li* (strength), namely,
the close integration of the several inner
elements within the human body. *Wai
San He* refers to the harmonies of the
shoulder with the hip, the elbow with the
knee, and the hand with the foot, namely,
the coordination of various body parts
in performing the technique. Therefore,
Xing Yi Quan is also known as the *Xin Yi
Liu He Quan* (The Six-Harmony Fists of
the Mind's Intent).

The unique characteristic of *Xing
Yi Quan* lie in the use of intent to lead
the move, the use of intent to lead *Qi*,
the use of *Qi* to induce force, and the
conversion of clumsiness to skills. Not
only does it emphasize the alternate
application of toughness and softness,
the accompaniment of *Yin* and *Yang*,
the changefulness between asthenia and
sthenia, and the cultivation of internal *Qi*
and internal strength, but it also advocates
pre-emptive tactics of delivering attacks
while the opponent is not yet prepared,
taking him down out of surprise via direct
aggression and rapid offense.

The stance of *Xing Yi Quan* is based
upon the *San Ti Shi* (tripartite) static

形意拳的特点是以意行事，以意领气，以气催力，化拙为巧。既讲究刚柔相济，阴阳相伴，虚实变化，注重对内气、内功的培养，又主张直取快攻，攻其不备，出其不意，先发制人。

形意拳桩法以三体式站桩为基础，三体式是按照形意拳动作要领设计的一种站桩姿势，是形意拳最重要的基本功。形意拳的各种拳路尽管变化万端，但都是以三体式这个基本姿势为基础，所以有"万法出于三体式"之说。

stance, which is designed in accordance with the movements of the *Xing Yi Quan*. Since it is the most important basic skill of *Xing Yi Quan*, all the fist fighting techniques and styles of *Xing Yi Quan*, no matter how changeable they are, are based upon this foundation of the *San Ti Shi* stance, hence the saying that "All styles originate from the *San Ti Shi* stance."

The most fundamental fist techniques of *Xing Yi Quan* are the *Wu Xing Quan* (Five Element Fists), which includes *Pi Quan* (Chop Fist), *Beng Quan* (Burst Fist), *Zuan Quan* (Drill Fist), *Pao Quan*

三体式站桩

三体式站桩把人体各部位按照形意拳的动作要领安排成一个圆满完整的姿势，基本要求是：两脚前后开立，全脚掌着地。前脚脚尖向前，后脚脚尖外展45度。两腿微屈，大腿斜向下，两膝微微内扣，两脚间距约一小腿长，重心偏于后退。

The *San Ti Shi* Stance

The *San Ti Shi* stance arranges various parts of the human body into a posture of a consummate circle in accordance with the essential movements of the *Xing Yi Quan*. The basic requirements include: Both feet are spread apart in the front and back, with the entire soles of the feet attached to the ground. The toes of the forefoot are facing forward while the toes of the back foot are angled outward by 45 degrees. The legs are bent, with the thighs slanting downward and the both knees slightly clamping toward each other. The distance between the two feet should be the length of the shin and the center of gravity is put a little backwards.

形意拳动作要领
Essential Moves of *Xing Yi Quan*

头向上顶，颈要竖直，下颏内收

The head is held up, with the neck upright and the chin held back.

胸部略向内含

The chest is slightly pumped.

两肩松垂，肘部下垂，塌腕，合掌

Drop the shoulders naturally, with the elbows drooped, the wrists down and palms joined.

腹部自然充实

The abdomen naturally filled.

上体正直，不俯不仰

The upper body should keep upright without leaning forward or backward.

塌腰收臀

Contract the waist, and draw back the hips.

屈膝微扣

The knees are bent and slightly clamped toward each other.

脚跟外撑，脚趾扣地

The heels are rooted, and the toes buckled to the ground.

形意拳最基本的拳法是五行拳，包括：劈拳、崩拳、钻拳、炮拳、横拳。形意拳的其他各种拳法多是由五行拳变化而来，所以五行拳也称"形意母拳"。

五行拳以中国传统文化中的五行学说命名。五行拳有劈、崩、钻、炮、横五式，分别对应金、木、水、火、土五行，五行之间相生相克的关系，可以用来说明五种拳法之间的相互转化和相互制约。

五行学说还把五行拳与健身联系起来。人体的内脏器官是一个有机联系的整体，各器官有着不同的生理特性，五脏六腑之间存在着生克制化的关系，可依据五行的观点来阐释。内脏与五行相对应，如肺

(Cannon Fist), and *Heng Quan* (Lateral Fist). All the varieties of other *Xing Yi Quan* techniques derive from this *Wu Xing Quan*. Thus, *Wu Xing* Quan is also known as the "Parent *Quan* of *Xing Yi*".

The *Wu Xing* Quan is named after the Five Elements Theory of the ancient Chinese culture. The five fist techniques of *Wu Xing Quan—Pi, Beng, Zuan, Pao* and *Heng*—correspond respectively to the five elements of metal, wood, water, fire and earth. The mutually beneficial and restrictive relationships among the five elements can serve to interpret the mutual transformation and restraint among the five fist techniques.

The *Wu Xing (Five Elements)* Theory also relates the *Wu Xing Quan* to physical fitness. The internal organs inside the human body compose a totality with organic interrelationships. Though each organ possesses different physiological properties, the relationships in the form of mutual *Sheng* (generation), *Ke* (elimination), *Zhi* (restriction), and *Hua* (transformation) exist among the

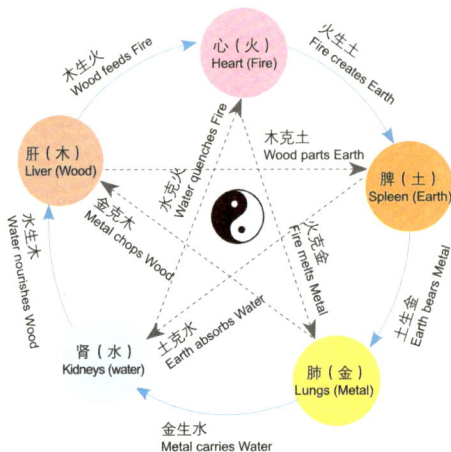

• 形意拳与五行及人体五脏六腑的关系图
Relationship Chart of the Five *Xing Yi Quan* in correspondence to the *Wu Xing* (Five Elements) and *Wu Zang Liu Fu (Internal organs)*.

- 劈拳
Pi Quan (Chop Fist)

- 炮拳
Pao Quan (Cannon Fist)

- 横拳
Heng Quan (Lateral Fist)

- 崩拳
Beng Quan (Burst Fist)

- 钻拳
Zuan Quan (Drill Fist)

属金、肝属木、肾属水、心属火、脾属土。因此，练五行拳有利于五脏：练劈拳可以养肺、练崩拳可以舒肝、练钻拳可以补肾、练炮拳可以保心、练横拳可以利脾。

十二形拳是形意拳基本的拳术套路之一。此拳模仿龙、虎、猴、马、鸡、鹞、燕、蛇、鼍（音同驼）、鸽、鹰、熊等十二种动物，根据动物的动作形态与技能编创而成。十二形拳象其形、取其意，生动、活泼、有趣、实用，出手生猛，具有鲜明的攻防特性。

five viscera and six bowels (*Wu Zang Liu Fu*) of human internal organs, which can be explained in the light of the *Wu Xing* Theory. Each internal organ corresponds to an element, such as lungs to metal, liver to wood, kidneys to water, heart to fire, and the spleen to earth. Therefore, the practice of the *Wu Xing Quan* will benefit the five organs, for example: The practice of *Pi Quan* can benefit the lungs, *Beng Quan* benefits the liver, *Zuan Quan* benefits the kidneys, *Pao Quan* benefits the heart, and *Heng Quan* benefits the spleen.

Shi Er Xing Quan (the Twelve-form Fist) is one of the fundamental fist fighting drills of the *Xing Yi Quan*. By imitating the twelve animals, namely the dragon, tiger, monkey, horse, rooster, hawk, swallow, snake, Chinese alligator, dove, eagle and bear, the Twelve-form Fist was created on the basis of the movements and skills of these animals. The Twelve-form Fist copies their forms and emulates their mindset to obtain distinct offensive and defensive characteristics that are vivid, lively, interesting, practical and fierce in delivery.

> 八卦掌

八卦掌全称"游身八卦连环掌"。八卦掌是以八卦为理论基础的一种以掌法变换和行步走转为主的拳术。八卦掌以自己的一个臂长的距离为半径画一个圆，然后沿着这个圆走圈。一圈八步，八个掌势，套路非常灵活。它将武功与导引、吐纳融为一体，内外兼修。八卦掌技法以实战为主，同时在强身健体上有独特的功效。

八卦掌的普及归功于清朝咸丰年间（1851—1862）的武术家董海川。八卦掌主要有两个流派：一个是以程廷华的龙爪掌为代表的程派，一个是以尹福的牛舌掌为代表的尹派。

八卦掌的运动特点是：一走、二视、三坐、四翻。这些特点成为发展身手的快捷性，特别是锻炼下

> *Ba Gua Zhang (Ba Gua Palm)*

The full name of *Ba Gua Zhang* (*Ba Gua Palm*) is Flowing-body *Ba Gua* Chain Palms. *Ba Gua Zhang* is a fist fighting technique with changeful palm skills and mobile footwork based upon the theory of *Ba Gua*. In practicing *Ba Gua Zhang*, one moves around a circle made up of the radius of the length of the arm. The whole circle takes eight steps and eight palm moves. The whole drill work is very agile and unfixed. It combines the martial arts with *Dao Yin* and *Tu Na* (breathing control) to contain both the internal and external cultivation. *Ba Gua Zhang* is typified by practical functions in fighting, while unique effects on physical strengthening and fitness are also achieved.

The popularity of *Ba Gua Zhang* can be attributed to martial artist Dong Haichuan during the reign of the Emperor Xianfeng

武术
Chinese Martial Arts

● 太极八卦图

八卦图是用来表示八卦方位的图形符
号，通常与太极图搭配出现。八卦的每
个图形有一定的方位，八种图形相互之
间有一定的对应关系和变化规律。八卦
掌就是按照太极八卦图来进行演练。

Diagram of *Tai Chi* and *Ba Gua*

It contains graphic symbols to show the eight
Ba Gua orientations. It usually comes with the
Tai Chi diagram. Every symbol of the *Ba Gua*
diagram has a specific orientation and there
is a certain relationship and transformation
rule between each symbol. The delivery and
working of *Ba Gua Zhang* is performed in
compliance with the principles of the diagram
of *Tai Chi* and *Ba Gua*.

肢力量的必要条件。八卦掌注重身
法的灵活性，要求练者在不断走圈
中，改变敌我之间的距离及方向，
避正击斜，伺机进攻；出手讲究随
机应变，发挥掌比拳和勾更灵活多
变的特性。

八卦掌在掌法上讲推、托、
带、领、搬、扣、劈、进、掖、
撞、削、塌；在劲力上要求刚柔相
济，沾粘连随，拧旋挣裹，沉实圆
活，注重腰力，寸劲爆发，也有人
称之为"揉掌法"；在步法上强调
行步趟泥，换式摆扣；在腿法上注
重底盘，注重桩法，多用暗腿；在
技法上讲究游身绕进，斜出正入，
走化沾打，脱身化影，背身击敌；

in the Qing Dynasty (1851-1862). *Ba Gua Zhang* is composed of two primary schools. One is the Cheng School, represented by Cheng Tinghua's *Long Zhua Zhang* (Dragon Claw Palm), and the other is the Yin School, represented by Yin Fu's *Niu She Zhang* (Ox Tongue Palm).

The movements of *Ba Gua Zhang* are characterized by: 1) *Zou* (walk); 2) *Shi* (look); 3) *Zuo* (sit); and 4) *Fan* (flip, or turn). These characteristics provide the required training conditions for developing shortcuts for the skills of the body and hands, especially the power of the lower limbs. *Ba Gua Zhang* attaches great importance to the agility of body movements. It requires the practitioner to always walk in the inner circle so that he can change the distance and direction from the opponent, avoid direct attacks while reversing in a diagonal direction, and wait to deliver opportunistic attacks. The delivery of attacks demands to be adapted to changing circumstances to give play to palm strikes instead of punches and hooks for its flexibility and versatility.

Ba Gua Zhang categorizes its palm moves as *Tui* (push), *Tuo* (drag), *Dai* (bring), *Ling* (lead), *Ban* (move), *Kou* (clasp), *Pi* (chop), *Jin* (advance), *Ye* (tuck), *Zhuang* (hit), *Xiao* (pare) and *Ta* (collapse). In terms of power, it requires the integrated usage of the soft and the tough so as to stick and adhere, or twist to break free. Flexibility in circular motions is emphasized for the waist power to deliver inch-burst power. It is for this reason that *Ba Gua Zhang* is also known as the *Rou Zhang Fa* (Rubbing Palm Technique). The footwork emphasizes *Tang Ni Bu* (Muddy Walk) with special attention paid to the turn and lock in switching moves. In terms of leg work, it focuses on low stance, the stance style utilized and the use of hidden kicks. Its techniques focus on the skills of the body maneuver, diagonal-out and direct-in, as well as spin-off steps with sticky punch,

* 八卦掌动作——青龙探爪

青龙探爪是八卦掌最有代表性的掌式，八卦掌的各式掌法均由此掌式变化而来。因此，掌握和练好青龙探爪是八卦掌独门功夫的要求。

Ba Gua Zhang Move—Blue Dragon Reaching out Claws

Qing Long Tan Zhua (Blue Dragon Reaching out Claws) is the most typical palm technique of *Ba Gua Zhang* and where all the other *Ba Gua* palm techniques evolve from. Therefore, the mastery and skillful delivery of *Qing Long Tan Zhua* will provide a concrete manifestation of the unique Kung Fu of *Ba Gua Zhang*.

在形象上讲究行走如龙，回转若猴，换式若鹰，三形兼备，舒展大方；在套路编排上以八大掌为主，即单换掌、双换掌、顺势掌、背身掌、转身掌、磨身掌、翻身掌、回身掌，连环变化。

八卦掌不仅有拳术，还有操练器械的技法：春秋刀、战身枪、连环剑、连环纯阳剑、连环蟠龙棍、五行棒、昆仑铲、八卦刀等。

• 八卦掌动作——狮子张口
Ba Gua Zhang Move—Lion Roar

coupled with shadow disengagement and back strikes. In terms of form, it dictates the practice of walking like a dragon, turning like a monkey, and changing moves like a hawk. These three forms combined will allow generous extending and stretching of the maneuver. The routine drill of the style utilizes eight major palm techniques as it basis, which are *Dan Huan* Palm (Single-change Palm), *Shuang Huan* Palm (Double-change Palm), *Shun Shi* Palm (Go-along Palm), *Bei Shen* Palm (Back-body Palm), *Zhuan Shen* Palm (Turn-around Palm), *Mo Shen* Palm (Body-grind Palm), *Fan Shen* Palm (Body-flip Palm), and the *Hui Shen* Palm (Body-return Palm). All the palm moves come in succession with inexhaustible changes.

Ba Gua Zhang has not only fist fighting techniques but also weapon techniques, such as the *Chun Qiu Dao* (Spring-autumn Blade), *Zhan Shen Qiang* (Warrior Body Spear), *Lian Huan Jian* (Chain Strike Sword), *Lian Huan Chun Yang Jian* (Chain-strike Pure-Yang Sword), *Lian Huan Pan Long Gun* (Chain-strike Dragon Staff), *Wu Xing Bang* (Five-element Cudgel), *Kun Lun Chan* (*Kunlun* Shovel), and *Ba Gua Dao* (*Ba Gua* Blade).

- 八卦掌动作——提膝腕打

  Ba Gua Zhang Move—Knee Lift with Wrist Attack

- 八卦掌动作——风轮劈掌

  Ba Gua Zhang Move—Windmill Chop

- 八卦掌动作——乌龙摆尾

  Ba Gua Zhang Move—Black Dragon Wagging Tail

- 八卦掌动作——推窗望月

  Ba Gua Zhang Move—Push Window to See Moon

异彩纷呈的拳术

A Kaleidoscope of Fist Fighting Techniques

> 象形拳

象形拳，又叫"仿生拳"。此拳术模拟动物的动作特征和形态，以及人的某些生活习性，并巧妙地融合了武术攻防技术。

模仿动物的形态是中国古代武术一直普遍存在的现象，但象形拳更加集中地把动物的动作与武术结合在一起，不仅能健身，对培养人的形象思维和艺术审美也有一定价值。

象形拳历史悠久，在春秋战国时期的《尚书》中有"百兽图"；著名医师华佗（？ –208）曾编创了五禽戏，可以视为象形拳的雏形。

象形拳中的动作和套路十分丰富，主要包括两类：一类是武术技击与模仿动物相结合的仿生拳术，主要有猴拳、鹰拳、蛇拳、螳

> *Xiang Xing Quan* (Imitation Boxing)

Xiang Xing Quan (Imitation Boxing), also known as *Fang Sheng Quan* (Animal-imitation Fist), imitates the characteristics and forms of animal behaviors and certain habits in people's lives and then

● 华佗像
Portrait of Hua Tuo

五禽戏

五禽戏是中国的一种传统健身方法，由模仿虎、鹿、熊、猿、鸟（鹤）五种动物的动作组成，由东汉医学家华佗创制。五禽戏是一种动静兼备、刚柔相济、内外兼练的仿生功法，长期练习五禽戏有治病养生、强身健体、延年益寿的功效。其健身效果被历代养生家称赞，在中国民间广为流传。

Wu Qin Xi (Five-animal Play)

Wu Qin Xi is a traditional Chinese health and fitness exercise created by Hua Tuo, a physician in the Eastern Han Dynasty (25-220). It imitates the movements of five animals: tiger, deer, bear, ape and bird (crane). *Wu Qin Xi* is an animal imitation exercise which combines the static and the dynamic, the soft and the tough, the internal and the external. A sustained long-term practice of *Wu Qin Xi* can cure illnesses, nurture life force, strengthen physical health and procure longevity. Its healthful effects have been recognized by health specialists in various dynasties and the exercise has been widely spread in the civilian society across China.

鹿戏
Deer Play

鸟戏
Bird Play

虎戏
Tiger Play

熊戏
Bear Play

猿戏
Ape Play

蝶拳、鸭形拳等；一类是模仿醉汉的各种醉姿完成的武术动作，如醉拳、醉棍、醉剑等。

猴拳

猴拳因模仿猴子的各种动作而得名。猴子活泼好动，动作灵敏多变，人们在很早以前就开始模仿猴子了。西汉时期就有了猴舞和猴拳，长沙马王堆汉墓出土的西汉帛画《导引图》上有"沐猴灌"的名目和图像，描绘的正是猴子的动作。关于猴拳的文字记载，首次出现在明代戚继光所著的《纪效新书·拳经》中，在郑若曾著的《江

cleverly blends them into offensive and defensive skills of martial arts.

Animal imitation has been a common phenomenon in Chinese martial arts since ancient times. *Xiang Xing Quan* consciously adopts animal movements and incorporates them into martial arts techniques in a more focused way. It can not only provide physical fitness, but also proves valuable in cultivating people's pictographic thinking and artistic beauty.

There is a long history behind *Xiang Xing Quan*. In *Book of History* of the Spring and Autumn Period (770 B.C. – 476 B.C.), the "Chart of a Hundred Beasts" is included. The great ancient Chinese physician, Hua Tuo (?-208), constituted the *Wu Qin Xi* (Five-

● 猴拳

猴拳以轻盈进攻为主，防守为辅。在嬉戏中向对方发难，使人防不胜防。

Monkey Fist

Monkey Fist utilizes light attacks with supplemented defense as its primary strategy. Attacks are launched in laughing and playful situations, making it difficult for opponents to defend.

南经略》中也有关于猴拳套路动作的记载；在少林武术中也有猴拳。

猴拳套路动作包括了猴子的基本动作，由出洞、窥望、看桃、攀登、摘桃、蹬枝、拼抢、藏桃、蹲坐、吃桃、喜乐、惊审、入洞等

animal Play), which can be regarded as the prototype of *Xiang Xing Quan*.

Xiang Xing Quan has a very rich repertoire of movements and drill forms. It is mainly divided into two categories. One is the imitation fist techniques that combine martial arts attached with animal movements, such as the Monkey Fist, Eagle Fist, Snake Fist, Mantis Fist and the Duck-shaped Fist. The other is the movements that imitate various postures of a drunken person, such as *Zui Quan* (Drunken Fist), *Zui Gun* (Drunken Staff) and *Zui Jian* (Drunken Sword).

Monkey Fist

The Monkey Fist was named for its imitation of various movements of monkeys. Monkeys are lively, active, nimble and versatile. People began imitating monkeys a long time ago. Monkey Dance and Monkey Fist were already there in the Western Han Dynasty (206 B.C.- 25 A.D.). In the silk painting of *Chart of Dao Yin* from the Western Han Dynasty, unearthed from the tomb at Mawangdui in Changsha, the item name and images of *Mu Hou Guan* (Monkey Bathing) precisely depicted the actions of a monkey. Written records of

• 猴拳
Monkey Fist

猿猴动作组成。猴拳模仿猴子的外形：耸肩、缩颈、圆背、束身、弯肘、垂腕、屈膝，动作形态可描述为：刚、柔、轻、灵、绵、巧、躲、闪、神、束。武术手法有抓、甩、采、切、刁、拿、扣、顶等。腿法有缠、蹬、踹、弹等。器械套路有猴棍、猴剑等。

猴拳内容繁杂，南北风格各异。南方重短打连发，北方则擅长刁钻巧击，但共同的特点是轻灵敏捷、刚柔相间、脆快有力、避重侧进、拳法密集。猴拳一般不主动攻击，避免与对方正面交锋，而是利用身灵步捷的躲闪，寻找机会，打击对手。

螳螂拳

螳螂拳是一种模仿螳螂动作形态的拳术。螳螂是一种食肉性的昆虫，两只巨大的前足上有锐利的锯齿，高举在胸前，在捕食猎物时，能够快速而准确地进行钳击。

螳螂的搏击方式给古代武术家很大的启发，他们据此编创了螳螂拳。螳螂拳分南北两派，南派螳螂拳是清代的周亚南编创的。北

the Monkey Fist first appeared in *Quan Jing* (Book of Fists) of Qi Jiguang's *New Book Recording Effective Techniques* in the Ming Dynasty (1368-1644). In Zheng Ruoceng's *Jiang Nan Management and Plans*, records associated with the drill works of Monkey Fist were also documented. The *Shaolin* Temple also has the Monkey Fist in its martial arts techniques.

The drill work (*Tao Lu*), or forms, of the Monkey Fist are composed of a series of basic monkey actions, including getting out of the cave, peeping, spotting peaches, climbing, peach plucking, jumping on branches, scrambling, hiding peaches, squatting, eating peaches, happiness, startled rush, and entering the cave. Monkey Fist also imitates the body movements of monkeys, such as shrugging shoulders, withdrawing the neck, arching the back, contracting the body, bending elbows, drooped wrists, and bending knees. Monkey's manners are also borrowed and summarized as being *Gang* (strong), *Rou* (soft), *Qing* (light), *Ling* (nimble), *Mian* (sustained), *Qiao* (delicate), *Duo* (hidden), *Shan* (dodging), *Shen* (alert), and *Shu* (restrained). Hand skills of the Monkey Fist include *Zhua* (catch), *Shuai* (throw),

● 螳螂拳
Mantis Fist

Cai (pluck), *Qie* (cut), *Diao* (trick), *Na* (take), *Kou* (clasp), *Ding* (prop) and so forth. Footwork includes bounding, treading, kicking, and springing. Weapon forms include the Monkey Staff and the Monkey Sword.

The Monkey Fist is complicated in content and differs greatly in the south and the north. The Southern Style emphasizes short punches in continuous attacks, while the Northern Style is more stressed in long crafty strikes. However, the common feature that both share is their agility, light movements, combination of soft and tough forces, clean shot in speed and power, weight dodging, and sideway approach. The sequence of the moves is compact and intense. The practice of Money Fist generally does not take the initiative to launch the offense. It avoids direct confrontation with the opponent. Instead, it makes use of nimble and spirited evasive techniques to look for a proper chance to strike the opponent.

Mantis Fist

The Mantis Fist is a martial arts technique that imitates the movements of a mantis. The mantis is a carnivorous insect with two large serrated forearms held high in

派螳螂拳由明末清初山东即墨县人王朗编创。王朗自幼喜欢练武，曾在少林寺学习武艺，偶然间受到螳螂捕蝉的启发，经过细心观察，逐渐总结出了勾、搂、采、挂、刁、黏、劈等武术技法，创编了北派螳螂拳。这种螳螂拳在北方流传很广，在长期传习中还形成了其他流派，如七星螳螂（又称"罗汉螳

• 螳螂拳
Mantis Fist

front of the chest. When hunting for food, it can quickly and accurately snatch its prey and deal a decisive blow.

The way the mantis fights offered great inspiration to ancient martial artists for their creation of the Mantis Fist. The Mantis Fist is divided into the Northern and Southern styles. The Southern style was created by Zhou Yanan during the Qing Dynasty (1644-1911), and the Northern style was formed by Wang Lang from the Jimo county of Shandong Province during the late Ming and early Qing dynasties. Wang Lang had had a liking for martial arts since his childhood. He was ever trained in the *Shaolin* Temple. He was perchance inspired by a scene of a mantis catching a cicada. After careful observation, he summed up the mantis skills of *Gou* (hook), *Lou* (hug), *Cai* (pluck), *Gua* (hang), *Diao* (trick), *Nian* (stick) and *Pi* (chop), and created the Northern-style Mantis Fist. This style was so widely practiced in north China that it gradually developed various schools after a long period of time. Some of these schools include the *Qi Xing* (Seven Stars) Mantis (also known as the *Luo Han* Mantis), *Mei Hua* (Plum Flower) Mantis (also known as the "*Tai Chi* Mantis"), and the *Liu He* (Six

鄉"）、梅花螳螂（又称"太极螳
螂"）、六合螳螂（又称"马猴螳
螂"）等。

螳螂拳的套路动作严谨，衔
接巧妙，长短并用，有很强的攻
击性。螳螂拳在动作发力时，身
体、手臂的晃动，又快又猛，具
有刚柔相济，刚而不僵，柔而不
软等特点。

蛇拳

蛇拳又称"蛇行拳"，是模
仿蛇的各种动作和形态，结合

• 蛇拳
Snake Fist

Harmonies) Mantis (also known as the
Ma Hou Mantis).

The Mantis Fist is well-organized
in its drill work. All moves are well and
skillfully interconnected, with short-range
and long-range techniques alternated
to achieve powerful aggression. When
delivering the power, the body and arms
will shake in such a way as to induce a
fierce and fast attack, characterized by
such properties that both the soft and
tough forces are coordinated and the
tough moves are strong but not stiff,
while the soft ones are supple but not
sloppy.

Snake Fist

The Snake Fist (*She Quan*), also known
as "*She Xing Quan*" (Snake-running
Fist), is a fist fighting technique that
combines the imitation of various snake
movements and attack techniques. Snake
Fist was already included in *Shaolin
Quan* and Southern Fist during the
Ming Dynasty (1368-1644). In the Qing
Dynasty, both *Xing Yi Quan* and *Ba Gua
Zhang* also had the snake styles. Snake
Fist is primarily practiced in Zhejiang,
Fujian, Guangdong, Sichuan, Hong
Kong, Taiwan and so on.

技击而创成的拳术。明代时少林拳、南拳属内已有蛇拳，清代的形意拳、八卦掌中也有蛇形。蛇拳主要流传于浙江、福建、广东、四川、香港、台湾等地。

蛇拳手型以蛇形掌为主，有穿、插、钻、按、劈、摆、挑等掌法，步型有弓步、马步、跪步、丁步等。动作特点是：刚柔相济，开合得宜。以柔劲为主，柔中有刚。上肢、身体要松柔，下肢要桩实灵活。蛇拳有较高的实用价值，实战时身体颤动，步法灵活，双手忽闪，用指抢喉，以掌插肋。发劲时常以声助势，以气促力，以目传神。

● 蛇拳
Snake Fist

The hand styles of the Snake Fist are based upon the snake-shaped palms, such as *Chuan* (pierce), *Cha* (plug), *Zuan* (drill), *An* (press), *Pi* (split), *Bai* (wave), *Tiao* (prick) and others. Its footwork includes the bow steps, horse steps, kneeling steps, and T-shaped steps. Its movements are characterized by the alternating use of toughness and softness, and proper opening and closure. Its strength is primarily based on softness, but toughness is hidden in it. The upper limbs and the torso must be relaxed and soft, while the stance (*Zhuang*) of the lower limbs should be firm and flexible. The Snake Fist has very high practical values. In actual combat, the body slightly waves, the footwork is nimble, and both hands flicker. Fingers are used to jab the throat and palms are applied to strike the ribs. When power is executed, vocal sound is used to boost the aggressiveness, *Qi* is exerted to urge the force, and eyes are used for psychological effects.

The drill work (*Tao Lu*) of the Snake Fist is primarily composed of such moves as the *Shen She Lian Yue* (Snake God Practicing with the Moon), *Jin She Lu Qi* (Golden Snake Rising on Land), *She Pan Tian Zhen* (Snake Coiling Innocence),

蛇拳的套路主要由神蛇练月、金蛇陆起、蛇蟠天真、白蛇喷沫、腾蛇走雾、角蛇应尾等动作组成。主要模仿的是蛇的盘旋、曲伸、吞吐等动作。蛇拳的器械有蛇行刀、蛇行剑等。

鹰爪拳

鹰爪拳是吸取鹰的形、意、搏击方法而成的拳术。此拳由清代河北雄县人刘仕俊所创，模仿鹰爪抓扣和鹰翼翻旋的动作创编而成，经过后世传人不断发展融合而成一支

• 鹰爪拳
Eagle Claw Fist

Bai She Pen Mo (White Snake Spitting Foam), *Teng She Zou Wu* (Rising Snake Moves in the Mist), and *Jiao She Ying Wei* (Horned Snake's Responding Tail) in imitation of the circling, extending, swallowing and tongue-hissing of the snake. The Snake Fist also includes weapon techniques such as the *She Xing Dao* (Snake-running Blade) and *She Xing Jian* (Snake-running Sword).

Eagle Claw Fist

The Eagle Claw Fist is a martial arts technique which drew its components from the eagle's *Xing* (form), *Yi* (intent), and fighting method. Created in the Qing Dynasty by Liu Shijun from Xiong county in Hebei Province, the Eagle Claw Fist imitated the snatching and wing-turning movements of the eagle, and gradually became a large sect after continuous developments and integrations by later generations through the ages. The Eagle Claw Fist was popular in Hebei, Beijing, Hunan, Hubei, Guangxi, Guangdong, Sichuan and elsewhere. It is also practiced in Southeast Asia, Europe, Latin America and so forth.

The Eagle Claw Fist features rich claw techniques in various acts of seizing, locking, catching and grabbing, delivered

较大的派系。鹰爪拳流行于河北、北京、湖南、湖北、广西、广东、四川等地，东南亚及欧、美等国也有习练。…

该拳的特点是：爪法丰富，抓扣擒拿，上下翻转，连环快速。姿势雄健，手眼犀利，身步灵活，发力刚爆。有拳歌曰："手如鹰爪上下翻，臂如鹰翅左右展。猛如金鹰扑小鸡，缓如苍鹰翔九天。疾如雀鹰赶飞雁，警如崖鹰伏山间……"练法讲究伏闪多变，急缓相间，眼到手到，意到力到。

in upward or downward turns at fast and continuous speed. It keeps vigorous body postures, maintains skillful hand-and-eye coordination, executes swift body movements and generates a powerful burst of force. A song of martial arts described it as thus: "Hands are turning up and down like the eagle's claws; arms are expanding left and right like the eagle's wings. It's as fast as a golden eagle's dive to snatch little chicks, as slow as the eagle's laborious soar through the high skies, as swift as geese chased asunder by sparrows and hawks, and as alert as an eagle's highland scout…" The practice of Eagle Claw Fist emphasizes swift changes by alternated slow and fast moves. The hands should sync with sight and power with intent.

武术
Chinese Martial Arts

• 鹰爪拳
Eagle Claw Fist

醉拳

醉拳又称"醉酒拳"、"醉八仙拳",是模仿醉汉动作的拳术。醉拳曾借鉴古代的醉舞,在明代末年就已经流传很广了。其拳行招走势模仿醉汉前俯后仰,东倒西歪,佯作醉态,在似倒非倒、半倾半斜中,顺势完成各种技击动作。人们形容它"头如波浪,手似流星,身如杨柳,脚似醉汉"。

醉拳将拳法、醉形、摔法融为一体,独树一帜。醉拳的特点

• 醉拳动作——饮酒亮相
Drunken Fist Move—Debut with Wine

Drunken Fist

Drunken Fist (*Zui Quan*), also known as the *Zui Jiu Quan* (Wine-drunk Fist) or *Zui Ba Xian Quan* (the Drunken Fist of the Eight Immortals), is a martial arts technique that mimics the movements of a drunk. It also borrowed some of its moves from the ancient *Zui Wu* (Drunken Dance). The Drunken Fist was already widely circulated in the late Ming Dynasty. The way it delivers its techniques and the manner it executes its footwork are like a drunken person, tumbling forward and waggling around. While the body is moving half-leaning, tilting or near-falling in emulation of the drunken state, skills are also performed and completed all along. People described its form as "The head moves like waves, hands like meteors, body like a willow twig, and feet like those of a drunk."

The Drunken Fist achieves its uniqueness through its fusion of martial arts techniques with drunken forms and wrestling techniques. The characteristics of the Drunken Fist can be summarized under just one word, "drunkenness". It utilizes the drunkenness as a potentiality to confuse the opponent, and to usher in the attacks. The appearance (*Xing*) is

异彩纷呈的拳术

A Kaleidoscope of Fist Fighting Techniques

八仙

八仙是民间传说中道教的八位神仙，即铁拐李、汉钟离、张果老、蓝采和、何仙姑、吕洞宾、韩湘子、曹国舅，各具法力。八仙分别代表着男、女、老、幼、富、贵、贫、贱。八仙所持的檀板、扇、拐、笛、剑、葫芦、拂尘、花篮等八件物品称为"八宝"。

The Eight Immortals

The Eight Immortals (*Ba Xian*) come from a Taoist folklore about the eight immortal gods, each having his or her own supernatural power. They are Tieguai Li, Han Zhongli, Zhang Guolao, Lan Caihe, He Xiangu, Lü Dongbin, Han Xiangzi, and Cao Guojiu. Each of them represents a certain attribute of human beings: man, woman, the old, the young, the rich, the noble, the poor, and the low-status. The eight weapons held by the eight immortals, including the *Tan Ban* (hardwood clapper), the fan, the crutches, the flute, the sword, the gourd, the duster, and the flower basket, are collectively known as The Eight Treasures.

- 《八仙图》黄慎（清）
Portraits of the Eight Immortals by Huang Shen (Qing Dynasty,1644-1911)

● 醉拳动作——醉汉摆腿
Drunken Fist Move—The Kick of a Drunk

在于一个"醉"字，似醉取势，以醉惑人，以醉进招，形醉意不醉，步醉心不醉。在格斗中以醉态麻痹对手，使其放松警惕，然后出其不意，攻其不备。

醉拳的技击要求眼、手、身、腿、步的配合。眼法有视、瞧、藐、瞟。手法有点、盖、劈、插、刁、拿、采、扣。身法有挨、撞、挤、靠。腿法有勾、挂、盘、剪、提、蹬、弹、缠。步法有提、落、

drunk, but the intent (*Yi*) is sober. The footwork follows that of a drunk, but not the heart. In actual combat, its drunken movements serve to paralyze opponents by loosening their alertness so that an unexpected attack can be delivered suddenly.

The technique of Drunk Fist demands coordination among the eyes, hands, body, legs and footwork. The eye techniques are *Shi* (gaze), *Qiao* (glance), *Miao* (belittling watch) and *Piao* (sidelong glance). The hand techniques include *Dian* (point), *Gai* (cover), *Pi* (chop), *Cha* (insert), *Diao* (trick), *Na* (hold), *Cai* (pick), and *Kou* (lock). The body moves are *Ai* (incline), *Zhuang* (collide), *Ji* (elbow) and *Kao* (lean). Leg techniques include *Gou* (hook), *Gua* (hang), *Pan* (coil), *Jian* (scissor), *Ti* (raise), *Deng* (tread), *Tan* (spring), and *Chan* (entangle). The footwork includes *Ti* (raise), *Luo* (drop), *Jin* (advance), *Che* (retreat), *Sui* (smash), *Ji* (strike), *Nian* (grind) and *Gai* (cover). The principles of Drunken Fist are the practice of a drunken form but a sober mind, fast hand-eye coordination, crisp footwork with an active center of gravity, looking in one direction while attacking another, and avoiding the strength while attacking

进、撤、碎、击、碾、盖等。用法讲究形醉意清，手疾眼快，步碎心活，指东打西，避实击虚。

醉拳的流行套路有醉八仙、太白醉酒、武松醉酒、燕青醉酒、鲁智深醉打山门等。近现代在醉拳的基础上又发展了醉剑、醉棍、醉枪，以及醉拳对打、醉汉戏猴等套路。相较偏重武术实用性的古老醉拳套路，现代醉拳套路更突出醉形醉态的表现性。

醉拳的动作难度很大，对人体的柔韧、协调、灵敏和应变能力等均有较高的要求。其动作都严格遵守醉拳的技击法则，其飘逸洒脱的外形则是经过长期训练而高度熟练的结果。

• 醉拳动作——醉汉出店
Drunken Fist Move—Drunken Exit

the weak point.

Popular Drunken Fist drill work includes *Zui Ba Xian* (the drunken Eight Immortals), *Taibai Zui Jiu* (Drunken Poet Taibai), *Wu Song Zui Jiu* (Drunken Tiger-fighter Wu Song), *Yan Qing Zui Jiu* (Drunken Wanderer Yan Qing), and *Lu Zhishen Zui Da Shan Men* (Drunken Monk Lu Zhishen Knocking the Mountain Gate). In modern times, Drunken Sword, Drunken Staff and Drunken Spear have also been developed on the basis on the Drunken Fist. Drill forms such as Drunk Sparring and Drunk's Monkey Play were also developed. Compared to the old Drunken Fist oriented toward practical application, the modern forms of Drunken Fist are highlighted in its expressiveness of drunkenness.

Most moves of Drunken Fist are very difficult to perform and demand high flexibility, coordination, agility and responsiveness from the practitioner. These movements also comply strictly with the fighting principles of the Drunken Fist. Its carefree and eased forms are but results from long-term and high-demanding training.

武艺高强的《水浒传》英雄

　　武松、燕青、鲁智深都是中国古典小说《水浒传》中的经典人物形象，都位列梁山108位好汉之中。武松武艺高强，勇猛非凡，行侠仗义，疾恶如仇，曾经在景阳冈上空手打死猛虎，"武松打虎"的事迹也在后世广为流传。燕青英俊潇洒，风流倜傥，多才多艺，会吹箫唱曲，又射得一手好箭。鲁智深性情刚烈如火，率直粗犷，爱憎分明，好抱打不平，勇而有谋，胆大心细。

Outlaws of the Marsh Heroes

Wu Song, Yan Qing and Lu Zhishen are all classical characters from the Chinese novel *Outlaws of the Marsh*, and are members of the 108 heroes in Liangshan Mountain. Wu Song is extremely skilled in martial arts. Extraordinarily brave, chivalric and anti-injustice, he once killed a tiger with his bare hands in Jingyanggang. The story of Wu Song Fights the Tiger has also been widely circulated through generations. Handsome, romantically suave and versatile, Yan Qing is very crafted in the arts of archery, flute and vocal art. Fierce in temperament, Lu Zhishen has a clear line drawn between love and hate for things, being straightforward but rough, brave but prudent, bold but cautious and inclined to grudge about injustice.

●《水浒传》版画
Print of *Outlaws of the Marsh*

> 南拳

　　南拳是流行于中国长江以南地区的一类拳种，主要流行于福建、广东、广西、湖南、湖北、江西、浙江等地，故称"南拳"。清代《小知录》中记载的拳种中就有"南拳"，南拳拳系在清代逐渐发展完善，并流传到海外。

　　南方人普遍身材比较矮小精悍，动作机敏灵活，肌肉爆发力强，因此讲究近身短打。南拳的总体风格是步稳、拳刚、势烈，少跳跃，多短拳，在发力时，大多要呼喝作声，吐气催力，以增强爆发力。

　　南拳的动作紧凑严密，威猛迅疾，手法灵活绵密，上肢及手型富于变化，体现出以小打大、

> *Nan Quan* (Fist Fighting of Southern Areas)

Nan Quan is a fist fighting technique which originated south of the Yangtze River of China and is popular in provinces like Fujian, Guangdong, Guangxi, Hunan, Hubei, Jiangxi and Zhejiang, hence its name Nan Quan, which literally means a fist fighting technique practiced in the south. *Nan Quan* was existent in the Qing Dynasty according to the record of *Xiao Zhi Lu*, a book on a wide range of topics written by Lu Fengzao in the Qing Dynasty, and became mature then and spread overseas henceforth.

　　As southerners are generally short but strong, which enables them to be extremely swift and flexible with great explosive strength of muscle, they stress short range and quick fight. The overall

南拳动作——抛拳
Nan Quan Move—*Pao Quan* (Swing Fist Fighting)

以巧打拙、以多打少、以快打慢的技击特色。南拳手法多样，一势多手，多用短拳，体现出"一寸短一寸险"的优势。上肢动作较多，把胸、背、肩、肘的劲力合在一起。再加上气沉丹田，腹肌紧缩，把全身的劲力都集中在腿部，通过腰部动作的传递，传递到手臂，打出的拳刚劲有力。南拳身体活动范围较小，强调步

style of *Nan Quan* is characterized by stable stances, quick and extensive punches, vigorous movements, few jumps, more short-range fist fighting and a vocal articulation that helps to generate power and boosts the explosive strength.

Nan Quan is also famous for its compact and fast movements, flexible and meticulous hand techniques, as well as changing forms of hands and upper limbs. With all those features, *Nan Quan* manifests small, clever, frequent and fast moves in fighting. It boasts diversified hand techniques, sometimes different hand techniques for only one posture, and often uses short-range punches, the advantage of which is reflected in the Chinese saying that "Shortened distance is doubled danger." In terms of its moving upper limbs, *Nan Quan* puts together strength in the chest, back, shoulders and elbows, coupled with the breath sunk to *Dan Tian* (the lower belly), and concentrates all the strength in the legs, which is later passed on to the arms through waist movements to generate vigorous punches. *Nan Quan* practitioners move within a relatively small range and are required to have low stances as stable as rooted trees, erect

法沉稳，要求像扎入地下的大树一样稳固，重心较低，下盘"稳如铁塔坐如山"。

南拳很少用腿，而拳法则十分丰富，这与北方武术形成鲜明的对比，北方人身材普遍比较高大，注重用腿，跳跃的动作很多。人们常用"南拳北腿"来形容南派、北派武术的区别。

towers and unshakable mountains.

Nan Quan rarely uses legs but abounds in punches. This stands in stark contrast with the martial arts practiced in northern China where tall northerners prefer to kick and jump. Therefore, people usually distinguish northern and southern martial arts with the phrase "*Nan Quan Bei Tui*" (southern fist and northern leg).

南派武术、北派武术

南派武术、北派武术是指中国武术拳种的地域风格，并非指具体的流派。南派，泛指在长江以南各地流传的拳种，其总体特点是重视桩步和拳法，主要是以手搏击，拳法密集紧凑，脚法少，步法坚实沉稳；北派泛指在长江以北及黄河流域传播的拳种，特点是重视用腿，腿法丰富，架势舒展，动作起伏明显，放长击远。

Southern and Northern Schools of Martial Arts

Martial arts are classified into southern and northern schools only by regional style instead of specific schools. Southern school refers to the fist techniques prevailing in the south of the Yangtze River that feature stable stances, compact punches and little footwork, mainly attacking with hands; northern school, on the other hand, refers to the fist techniques spreading in the north of the Yangtze River and along the Yellow River that highlight footwork, a rich variety of kicks, extended postures, and conspicuous undulating movements for long-range fights.

• 南拳动作——骑龙步
Nan Quan Move—*Qi Long Bu*
(Riding Dragon Stance)

异彩纷呈的拳术

A Kaleidoscope of Fist Fighting Techniques

• 南拳动作——虚步
Nan Quan Move—*Xu Bu*
(Empty Step)

• 南拳动作——跪步
Nan Quan Move—*Gui Bu*
(Squatting Step)

南拳种类繁多，流传最广的有广东的五大名拳，即洪家拳、刘家拳、蔡家拳、李家拳、莫家拳，以及福建的咏春拳、五祖拳、鹤拳、罗汉拳等；湖南、湖北、江西等地流行的是邬家拳。

洪家拳又称"洪拳"，位居广东五大拳之首。相传由福建漳州人洪熙官所创。此拳在广东流行甚广，在东南亚一些国家和地区也

• 南拳动作——独立步

Nan Quan Move—*Du Li Bu* (Single Leg Stance)

Nan Quan falls into many categories, with the most famous being the five family styles of *Hong Jia Quan*, *Liu Jia Quan*, *Cai Jia Quan*, *Li Jia Quan* and *Mo Jia Quan* in Guangdong Province, *Wing Chun*, *Wu Zu Quan* (Five-ancestors Fist), *He Quan* (Crane Fist) and *Luo Han Quan* (Arhat Fist) in Fujian Province, and *Wu Jia Quan* in Hunan, Hubei and Jiangxi Provinces.

Hong Jia Quan, also known as *Hong Quan*, comes first among the five Guangdong family styles. Legend has it that it was founded by Hong Xiguan, a martial arts master from Zhangzhou, Fujian Province. This punching technique is popular in Guangdong and influential in some Southeast Asian countries and regions. *Hong Quan* routines are complicated with fists in a single form of dragon, tiger, lion, leopard, snake, crane, elephant, horse or monkey, and fists in mixed forms of *Hu He Shuang Xing Quan* (double animals of tiger and crane), *Wu Xing Quan* (five animals of dragon, tiger, leopard, snake and crane) or *Shi Xing Quan* (ten animals of dragon, tiger, lion, leopard, snake, crane, horse, eagle, bear and monkey). *Hong Quan* is featured by its simple yet forceful movements, few kicks, diversified hand techniques, stable

颇有影响。洪拳的拳械套路繁多复杂，有单形拳术，如龙拳、虎拳、狮拳、豹拳、蛇拳、鹤拳、象拳、马拳、猴拳、虎拳等；有混合形拳术，如虎鹤双形拳、五形拳、十形拳等。洪拳的特点是：动作刚劲有力，朴实浑厚。手法丰富，腿法较少，步稳势烈。含蓄发劲，先收后放。因势发声，以声助威。

广东五大名拳在发展中相互融合，如集蔡家拳、李家拳、佛家拳三家之长的蔡李佛拳，此拳在广

A Kaleidoscope of Fist Fighting Techniques

异彩纷呈的拳术

• 南拳动作——单蝶步

Nan Quan Move—*Dan Die Bu* (Single Butterfly Step)

and extensive steps. The practitioners usually first conserve power for a later outburst and natural vocal articulation for enhancement is used.

In their development, the five Guangdong Province family styles integrate with one another, thus giving birth to contemporary martial arts variants like Choi Lei Fut, a combination of *Cai* (Choi) *Jia Quan*, *Li* (Lei) *Jia Quan* and *Fo Jia Quan.* Choi Lei Fut is widely practiced in Guangzhou, Foshan, Hong Kong, Macao and Southeast Asia. Its characteristics lie in its flexible, swift and extended movements, with softness and toughness complementing each other to deliver bold and wise techniques. Its hand techniques are dominated by fists, palms and forearms, with a focus on coordination between attacks and defense with agile steps and a stable stance.

Wing Chun is one of the most famous fist techniques of *Nan Quan* that prevailed in Guangdong and Fujian in its early days. Named after its founder, the young woman Yim Wing-chun (also known as *Wing Chun San Niang*) from Fujian, *Wing Chun* has the following characteristics: It is applicable to actual combat with changing moves, simple movements, agile and changing

州、佛山、香港、澳门等地流传，在东南亚一带也较盛行。其特点是动作灵巧迅捷，舒展大方，刚柔相济，勇猛机智，手法以拳、掌、桥为主，注重攻防配合，步法灵活而稳健。

　　咏春拳是南拳中比较有名的拳术之一，早年流行于广东、福建各地。此拳由福建严咏春（又名"咏春三娘"）所创，故名"咏春拳"。咏春拳的特点是：立足于实

handwork, use of legs and hands in unison and inconspicuous leg attacks, and elbows are kept close to the body for protection of the centerline. Bruce Lee, a famous contemporary martial arts film actor, was a *Wing Chun* practitioner

- 咏春拳动作——右枕手
Wing Chun Move—*Yo Jam Sau* (Right Sinking Hand)

- 咏春拳动作——左摊手
Wing Chun Move - *Jo Taan Sau* (Left Opening Hand)

战，招式多变，动作朴素，手法灵活，丰富多变，起脚必配手，发腿隐蔽，出手护中。当代著名武打明星李小龙就从小练习咏春拳，后来他创立的截拳道就吸取了咏春拳的许多招式。

from an early age and founder of the *Jeet Kune Do* (the way of the intercepting fist) based on *Wing Chun* in his later life.

李小龙

　　李小龙(1940-1973)，著名武术技击家，世界武功片电影表演家，截拳道的创始人。他13岁时跟随名师叶问系统地学习咏春拳，此外，还练过洪拳、白鹤拳、谭腿、少林拳等。除了勤练中国拳法，李小龙还研究西洋拳的拳法，这些都为他后来自创截拳道打下了基础。

　　李小龙对现代武术和电影表演艺术的发展作出了巨大贡献。他曾参与拍摄的《唐山大兄》、《精武门》、《猛龙过江》、《死亡游戏》和《龙争虎斗》等功夫片风行海内外，中国功夫也随之闻名世界。他先后在1972年和1973年两度被国际权威武术杂志《黑带》评为世界七大武术家之一。美国报刊把他誉为"功夫之王"，日本人称他为"武之圣者"，香港报纸赞誉他为"当代中国武术及电影史上的奇才"。

● 李小龙与师父叶问切磋武艺
Bruce Lee and His Master Yip Man Are Exchanging Martial Arts Techniques.

Bruce Lee

Bruce Lee (1940-1973) was a famous martial arts boxer, international martial arts film actor and founder of the *Jeet Kune Do*. He started to systematically learn *Wing Chun* from Master Yip Man at 13. In addition, he also learned *Hong Quan*, *Bai He Quan* (white crane fist), *Tan Tui* (a leg technique created in the *Longtan* Temple) and *Shaolin Quan* and studied western fist techniques, which laid the foundation for his later founding of the *Jeet Kune Do*.

Bruce Lee has made a great contribution to the development of modern martial arts and the art of performance in the film industry. He starred in popular martial arts films like *The Big Boss*, *Fist of Fury*, *Way of the Dragon*, *Game of Death* and *Enter the Dragon* while making Chinese Kung Fu renowned to the rest of the world. He was twice honored as one of the seven martial arts masters by *Black Belt*, the world's leading magazine of martial arts, in 1972 and 1973. In 1972, he was elected one of the top 10 movie stars in Hong Kong. Besides, he was also reputed as the King of Kung Fu by American newspapers, *Saint of Martial Arts* by Japanese people and a "wizard in the modern history of Chinese martial arts and film" by Hong Kong newspapers.

- 李小龙
  Bruce Lee

> 长拳

长拳是中国武术的主要拳种之一，"长拳"一词最早见于明代戚继光所著的《纪效新书》："古今拳家，宋太祖有三十二势长拳"。现代新编长拳是在中华人民共和国成立后，吸取了诸拳种之长，把手型、手法、步型、步法、腿法、平衡、跳跃等基本动作规格化，按照长拳运动方法创编而成，使之成为基础武术训练和全国武术

> *Chang Quan* (Long-style Fist Fighting)

Chang Quan is one of the major fist techniques of Chinese Martial Arts. The phrase *Chang Quan* first appeard in *New Book Recording Effective Techniques*, a book written by the Chinese general Qi Jiguang in the Ming Dynasty (1368-1644), in the statement that "Among pratitioners in the past and present, Emperor Taizu of the Song Dynasty excells with his 32 *Chang Quan* techniques." Modern *Chang Quan* came into being after the founding of

• 长拳动作——仆步亮掌
Chang Quan Move—*Pu Bu Liang Zhang* (Flash Palm with Squatting Stance)

• 长拳动作——仆步抡劈拳
Chang Quan Move—*Pu Bu Lun Pi Quan*
(Chop Fist with Squatting Stance)

表演比赛项目。

　　长拳的特点是姿势舒展大方，动作灵活快速，出手或出腿时以放长击远为主，有时还配合拧腰顺肩来加长击打点，以发挥"长一寸强一寸"的优势。

　　长拳的套路动作数量和趟数一般较多，长拳中也间或使用短拳，但整套动作是以长击动作为主，动作刚柔相济，快慢相间，节奏分明。长拳的基本技法规律包括：顶头竖脊，舒肢紧指（趾）；形合力顺，动迅静定；以眼传神，以气助势；阴阳相依，相辅相成。

　　长拳的手法主要有冲、劈、崩、贯、砸等拳法，推、挑、撩、劈、砍等掌法，顶、盘、格等肘法。腿法主要有弹、蹬、踹、点、铲、踢、里合、外摆、拍、扫等。还有各种摔法、拿法、跳跃、平衡等。

the People's Republic of China. It is created in accordance with the exercise modes of *Chang Quan* by drawing upon the merits of various fist techniques and standardizing some basic movements such as hand forms, hand techniques, steps, footwork, kicks, balances and jumps. Now, *Chang Quan* is included in the basic martial arts training and an event in the national martial arts performance and contests.

Chang Quan is featured by its stretched and natural postures, and agile and quick movements. It focuses on long-range hand or leg attackes. Sometimes, it lengthens the attack distance by twisting the waist and inclining the shoulders in coordination to leverage the advantage that "lengthened distance means fortified strength."

Despite its many routines and combinations with short range puches in

長拳动作——弓步冲拳
Chang Quan Move—*Gong Bu Chong Quan* (Thrust Punch with Bow Stance)

長拳动作——歇步抡砸拳
Chang Quan Move—*Xie Bu Lun Za Quan* (Hammer Fist with Resting Stance)

some cases, *Chang Quan* mainly focuses on long range fighting with soft and tough actions, and rhythmed slow and quick movements. Basic laws in practicing *Chang Quan* include: Hold your head high and staighten your back, relax your limbs and tighten your fingers (toes); coordinate your forms and generate power smoothly, move quickly and hold still; use eyes to convey spirits, use breath to add to strength; and *Yin* and *Yang* are interdependent and complementary.

Hand techniques of *Chang Quan* are mainly punches like *Chong* (thrust fist), *Pi* (chop fist), *Beng* (crushing/smashing punch), *Guan* (sweeping side punch) and *Za* (hammer fist); palm techniques like *Tui* (push), *Tiao* (upward push), *Liao* (upward cut), *Pi* (splitting palm) and *Kan* (horizontal chop); elbow techniques like *Ding* (elbow thrust), *Pan* (hook) and *Ge* (parry). Its major kicks include *Tan* (thrust kick), *Deng* (heel kick), *Chuai* (sole kick), *Dian* (point kick), *Chan* (edge kick), *Ti* (toe kick), *Li He* (inside crescent), *Wai Bai* (outside crescent), *Pai* (pat kick) and *Sao* (sweep kick). There are also various wrestling, catching, jumping and balancing moves.

> 翻子拳

翻子拳，又称"翻子"或"翻拳"，是中国武术中的一个优秀拳种。翻子拳在明代已很有影响，戚继光在《纪效新书·拳经·捷要篇》中提到的"八闪拳"，就是现在所说的翻子拳，戚继光说它"善之善者也"，可谓赞誉备至。

翻子拳又被称做"八闪翻"，是根据它有前、后、左、右、上、下、中、双等八种闪翻技法而定名的。"闪"是说翻子拳的拳势迅疾如闪电，又闪摆不定，令人难以提防。"翻"是指上肢的翻转动作多，上而翻下，下而翻上，左右相顾，前后兼施，翻生不息。

翻子拳的流传与少林武术有一定关系。据说，少林僧人曾把此拳传授给了河北高阳的段氏，段氏一

> *Fanzi Quan* (Flash Fist Fighting)

Fanzi Quan, also known as *Fanzi* or *Fan Quan*, is an excellent fist technique of Chinese martial arts. It has been influential since the Ming Dynasty and the *Ba Shan Quan* (eight flash tumbles) mentioned in the *Jie Yao* chapter of *Quan Jing* (Book of Fists) of *New Book Recording Effective Techniques* is today's *Fanzi Quan*, which was thought of highly by the author Qi Jiguang as being the most skillful martial art of all time.

Fanzi Quan is also called *Ba Shan Fan* for its eight flash tumbles, including front, back, left, right, up, down, middle and double tumble techniques. *Shan* refers to the punches that move as quickly as flashes of lightning and attack people in an unpredictable manner, leaving them no time to react; *Fan* refers to the continuous tumbles of upper limbs, first

● 翻子拳
Fanzi Quan

● 翻子拳
Fanzi Quan

家为了防身自卫，把此拳世世代代传了下来。后来，翻子拳又传入辽宁、甘肃、陕西等地，形成了不同流派。翻子拳在西北、东北地区传播较广，虽然同属一脉，但风格上略有不同。例如，西北地区的翻子拳注重以腰发力，动作浑厚；东北地区的翻子拳，动作脆快。

翻子拳的套路一般短小精悍，发力迅猛，拳法又紧又快，打起来

downward, then upward, then downward again while balancing the left and right and the front and back.

The circulation of *Fanzi Quan* is related to *Shaolin* Martial Arts to a certain degree. It is said that a *Shaolin* monk once taught it to the Duan family in Gaoyang, Hebei Province, who passed it down from generation to generation for the sake of self-defense. Later, *Fanzi Quan* spread to Liaoning, Gansu and Shaanxi Provinces, where it developed

如风驰电掣，密集如雨，架势俯伏闪动，动作迅猛而轻灵，像放鞭炮一样，势如破竹。所以拳谚称"双拳密如雨，脆快一挂鞭"。翻子拳在技击时，以腰力贯穿其身法，侧进斜击，脚不过膝，动作朴实无华，非常实用。

into different schools. Northwestern *Fanzi Quan* and northeastern *Fanzi Quan* share the same origin with slightly different styles. To illustrate, *Fanzi Quan* in northwestern China emphasizes vigorous movements and power from the waist while that in northeastern China emphasizes direct and quick movements.

Fanzi Quan routines are short and concise which feature swift and explosive strength, compact punches quick as lightning and thick as raindrops, bending and flashing postures, and light movements as unexpected as the setting off of firecrackers and vigorous like the splitting of bamboo, hence the proverb on punches: "Two punches are as thick as raindrops and unexpected as the setting off of firecracker strings." In fist fighting, *Fanzi Quan* generates power form the waist, attacks sideways, keeps feet lower than the knees, and moves in a simple manner and is proved to be very effective.

> 戳脚

　　戳脚是一种以腿脚功夫为主的拳术，有"北腿之杰"之称。在中国古代武术中，武术家一般比较忌讳用腿，出腿都非常谨慎，有"动腿三分虚"之说。因为腿不仅起到支撑全身重量的作用，还要根据格斗需要，完成闪跳腾挪的任务。但是戳腿一反常规，在技击中主要靠腿脚打人，充分发挥了腿的威力。腿比手臂长，力量大，在格斗时人们往往注意上肢动作，而忽视了下肢，所以用腿攻击有出其不意、攻其不备的效果，戳脚正是利用了腿的这个优势。

　　戳脚起源于宋代，盛行于明清。中国古典小说《水浒传》里，对武松醉打蒋门神做了精彩的描写："武松先把两个拳头去蒋门神

> *Chuo Jiao* (Poking the Feet)

Chuo Jiao (literally meaning poking the feet) is a fist fight technique that emphasizes kicks and footwork and is reputed as The Best of *Bei Tui*. In ancient Chinese Martial Arts, masters were very discreet in using their legs as it might reduce the chance of winning because legs should support the whole body and fulfill jumping and moving tasks as required in a fight, hence the saying that "A move in the leg produces deficiency to some extent". However, *Chuo Jiao* is unconventional in that it wins fights by capitalizing the force of feet and legs. Legs are longer and more powerful than arms, and people in fighting usually pay too much attention to their upper limbs to neglect the lower limbs so that fighting with legs can take the opponent by surprise. That is exactly what *Chuo Jiao* is about.

戳脚
Chuo Jiao

脸上虚影一影，忽地转身便走。蒋门神大怒，抢将来，被武松一飞脚踢起，踢中蒋门神小腹上，双手按了，便蹲下去。武松一趸（音同穴），趸将过来，那只右脚早踢起，直飞在蒋门神额角上，踢着正中，往后便倒。武松追入一步，踏住胸脯……"武松使用的打法正是戳脚中的招法，称作"玉环步、鸳鸯脚"。近代，戳脚主要流传于华北地区，据传太平军中有一位名叫赵灿益的战将，精通戳脚。太平军北伐失败后，赵灿益就隐姓埋名，在河北一带传授戳脚，使戳脚流传开来。

戳脚以腿见长，主要有踢、蹬、提、圈、掀、点、插、摆八

Chuo Jiao originated in the Northern Song Dynasty (960-1127) and acquired ascendancy during the Ming and Qing dynasties (1368-1911). An example of *Chuo Jiao* can be found in *Outlaws of the Marsh*, one of the Four Great Classical Novels of Chinese literatures, in its vivid description of how drunken Wu Song beat Jiang the Gate Guard:

Wu Song flourished his two fists at Jiang's face, then suddenly turned and started away. Enraged, Jiang raced after him. Wu Song lashed out backwards with his left foot and kicked him in the groin. As Jiang clasped his injured section and doubled over in pain, Wu Song whirled around and swung his right foot in a flying kick to the forehead that slammed the big man over on his back. Wu Song planted one foot on his chest and ... (An excerpt from *Outlaws of the March* written by Shi Nai'An and translated by Sidney Shapiro)

The fighting techniques Wu Song used belong to *Chuo Jiao*, namely *Yu Huan Bu* and *Yuan Yang Jiao* (step of a nephrite ring and leg of a mandarin duck). *Chuo Jiao* was mainly practiced in modern northern China, and Zhao Canyi, a general in the Taiping Army who was said to be a *Chuo Jiao* master, taught

● 《水浒传之醉打蒋门神》版画
Print of *Drunken Wu Song Beating Jiang the Gate Guard*

种基本腿法，在此基础上变化出八十一个腿法。戳脚强调手脚并用的技击方法，但有主次之分，先以手臂动作迷惑对手，再用腿发起攻击。有人将这种独特的技击方法描述为"手是两扇门，全凭腿打人"，"手打三分，脚踢七分"。

戳脚有文趟子、武趟子两种类型。武趟子是戳脚的本源，动作舒

Chuo Jiao in Heibei Province incognito after the defeat of the northern expedition of the Taiping Army. Thus, *Chuo Jiao* was spread to the rest of China.

Chuo Jiao outstands in its kicks and has developed 81 kick techniques based on the eight fundamental kicks of *Ti* (kick), *Deng* (tread), *Ti* (lift), *Quan* (circle), *Xian* (lift up), *Dian* (point), *Cha* (pierce) and *Bai* (swing). *Chuo Jiao* emphasizes the collaborative use of fists and feet with different focuses: First, confuse the opponent with hand movements and then attack the opponent with legs. People describe this unique fighting method as "fist deceives and foot attacks" or "victory equals 30% of hand techniques and 70% of leg movements."

Chuo Jiao is *classified into Wen Tangzi* and *Wu Tangzi*, the latter constituting the root of *Chuo Jiao*. *Wu Tangzi* focuses on training of leg and foot techniques characterized by extended and powerful movements, long-range-fighting oriented, and softness and toughness with toughness as the major player. *Wu Tangzi* routines are named *Jiu Zhuan Lian Huan Yuan Yang Jiao* (mandarin duck leg with nine chained turns): *Jiu Zhuan* in that it has nine interchangeable kick techniques; *Lian Huan* in that each kick technique is

展大方，刚健有力，放长击远，刚中带柔，以刚为主，习练的重点是腿法、脚功。武趟子套路叫"九转连环鸳鸯脚"，有九路腿法，各路可转换练习，故称"九转"。每路腿法都是一步一脚，连连发出，环环相套，故称"连环"；发腿一左一右，腿、脚连环出击，左右互换，故称"鸳鸯脚"。

文趟子由武趟子演化而来，动作小巧明快，节奏紧凑，灵活善变，柔中寓刚，绵里藏针，其练法是心到神到，手到脚到。文趟子套路叫"八根"，包括转脚、走外、玉环步、蹶子腿、开步雷、似箭手、五花炮、十字捶。腿法要求短腿低踢，手脚齐用。

delivered in one step in succession and inter-connected; and *Yuan Yang Jiao* in that each move of the left leg and foot is accompanied by that of the right leg and foot, and vice versa.

Wen Tangzi is evolved from *Wu Tangzi* and is flexible and changing with compact and swift movements, tight rhythm, softness embodied in toughness and a firm character behind a gentle appearance. The secret in practicing *Wen Tangzi* is for the hands and feet to follow the mind. *Wen Tangzi* routines are called *Ba Gen* (eight steps), including *Zhuan Jiao* (turning of feet), *Zou Wai* (walking outward), *Yu Huan Bu* (steps in resemblance of jade rings), *Juezi Tui* (backward kick), *Kai Bu Lei* (starting steps like a thunder), *Si Jian Shou* (arrow-like hands), *Wu Hua Pao* (five-flower cannon fist) and *Shi Zi Chui* (cross-shaped hammer), all requiring recovering legs and lowering kicks with the combined use of hands and feet.

十八般兵器

Eighteen Weapons of Chinese Martial Arts

器械武术是传统武术的重要组成部分。武术中使用的器械种类繁多，人们常用"十八般兵器"或"十八般武艺"作为中国器械武术的统称，泛指使用各种器械的多种武艺。武术器械门类众多，各有所长，其使用方法和用途也各不相同，下面介绍几种现代武术常用的器械。

Weapon martial arts is an integral part of traditional martial arts. A rich variety of weapons are used in martial arts and people usually use "eighteen weapons" or "eighteen martial arts" as an umbrella name for the Chinese weapon martial arts and to refer to the various martial arts with various weapons. Such weapons are divided into numerous schools with distinctive strengths and used in different ways for different purposes. Below are some modern weapons in common use.

• 镋
Fork-like Weapon with a Long Sharp Tip

十八般兵器

用于武术演练的器械，主要由古代冷兵器发展演化而来。冷兵器在明代发展到了顶点，门类齐全、品种繁多的冷兵器为器械武术的发展提供了条件。

古代冷兵器原本都是在实际作战中被广泛使用，有的最初甚至是农具，但大多在后来的发展过程中成为用于防身、演练武艺的器械。十八般武艺的出现满足了社会观赏、个人防卫及健身的需要。

关于十八般兵器，历代记述不尽相同，以握柄范围的长短作为区分，有"九长九短"（九种长兵器、九种短兵器）之说。所谓"九长"，是指枪、戟、棍、钺、叉、镋、钩、槊、环；"九短"是指刀、剑、拐、斧、鞭、铜、锤、棒、杵。古人所说的"短兵相接"，就是指拿着"九短"之类的兵器格斗。每一类兵器又各有许多形制及功能不同的器械。如"刀"类，有九环刀、雁翎刀、春秋刀、三尖两刃刀、斩马刀、砍山刀、大刀等等，名目繁多。在现代武术中，器械有很多种，最常用的是刀、枪、剑、棍。

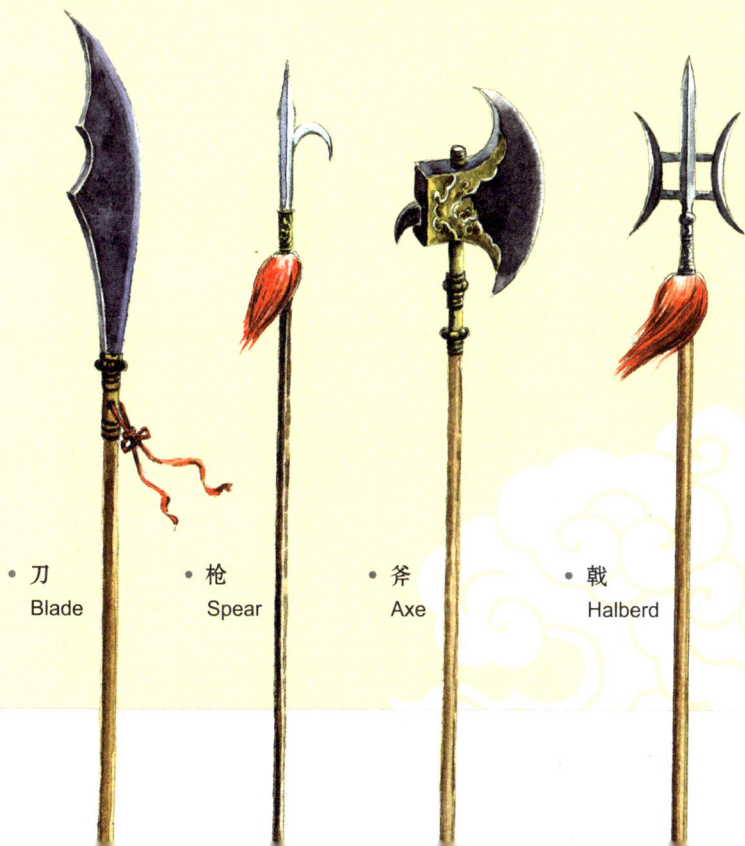

- 刀
  Blade

- 枪
  Spear

- 斧
  Axe

- 戟
  Halberd

Eighteen Weapons of Chinese Martial Arts

Weapons for martial arts drills mainly derive from ancient cold weapons, which reached its peak in the Ming Dynasty (1368-1644) and laid a good foundation for the later development of martial arts weapons with a wide range and rich variety.

Ancient cold weapons were originally extensively used in actual combat, some of which were even farm tools, but in later development, most of them became weapons for self-defense and martial arts practice. The appearance of the eighteen martial arts weapons satisfies the demands of social appreciation and individual self-defense and body-building.

Historical records differ from one another in the eighteen martial arts weapons. By length of handles, martial arts weapons are differentiated as *Jiu Chang Jiu Duan* (nine long-handled weapons and nine short-handled weapons). To be more specific, *Jiu Chang* refers to spear, halberd, staff, broadaxe, fork, fork-like weapon with a long sharp tip, hook, long spear and ring while *Jiu Duan* refers to blade, sword, crutch, axe, whip, mace, hammer, club and pestle. *Duan Bing Xiang Jie* in the words of Chinese ancestors is what is known as fights with *Jiu Duan* weapons. Each category has under its name weapons of different forms and functions. For example, under the blade category, there are *Jiu Huan Dao* (nine ring blade), *Yan Ling Dao* (goose-quill saber), *Chun Qiu Dao* (spring-and-autumn blade), *San Jian Liang Ren Dao* (triple-pointed and double-bladed saber), *Zhan Ma Dao* (horse chopping saber), *Kan Shan Dao* (mount cutting saber), and *Da Dao* (Chinese great blade). In mordern martial arts, blade, spear, sword and staff are the most commonly used weapons.

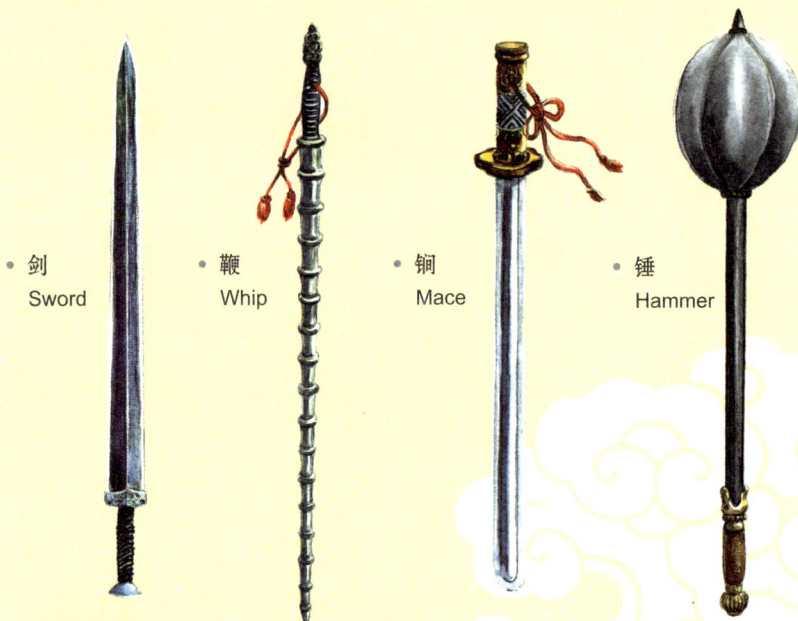

- 剑
  Sword

- 鞭
  Whip

- 锏
  Mace

- 锤
  Hammer

> 刀

刀是武术中最常用的器械之一，为十八般兵器之首。刀是一种单面长刃的短兵器，有"百兵之胆"的美称。

刀由刀尖、刀身、刀刃、刀背、护手、刀把组成。刀尖、刀刃是最锋利的部位，主攻；刀背坚固宽厚，主防。刀有长刀、短刀、斩马刀、朴刀、钩刀、眉刀、匕首刀、三尖两刃刀、飞刀之分，又有单刀、双刀、藏刀之别。

刀有劈、砍、割、捅的功能，勇猛彪悍，素有"刀如猛虎"之说。古时士卒短兵相接，以用刀者居多。刀法以劈和砍为基本动作，在此基础上，历代用刀习武之人总结出了多套刀法，并配合各种步型、步法等动作构成套路。现存的

> Blade

The blade is one of the most commonly used weapons in martial arts and ranks at the top among the eighteen martial arts weapons. It is a bladed weapon with a short hilt and praised as the "gut of all weapons".

A blade is composed of the blade point, body, edge, fuller, guard and grip. Point and edge, the sharpest of all parts, are responsible for attacks; fuller, the most solid and thickest part, is in charge of defense. In the subdivision of blade, there are long blade, cutlass, horse chopping blade, long-hilt blade, hook blade, eyebrow-shaped knife, dagger, triple-pointed and double-bladed saber and flying blade. It can also be classified into single blade, double blade and hidden blade.

The blade can split, chop, cut and stab, and its powerfulness renders it the

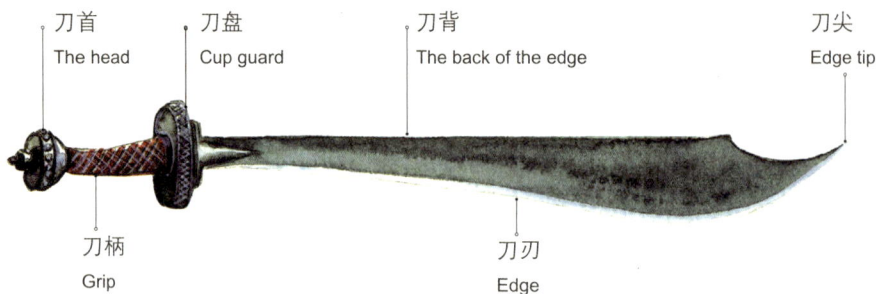

刀首　　　　　刀盘　　　　　　刀背　　　　　　　　　　　　　刀尖
The head　　　Cup guard　　　The back of the edge　　　　　　Edge tip

刀柄　　　　　　　　　　　　　　　　　刀刃
Grip　　　　　　　　　　　　　　　　　Edge

- 刀的结构示意图
  Sketch Map of Blade Structure

刀法派别有太极刀、梅花刀、八卦刀、八门金锁刀、日月乾坤刀、少林双刀十八滚等。

- 太极刀法的练习者 (图片提供: FOTOE)
  Practitioner of *Tai Chi Dao*

name of a fierce tiger. In ancient times, most soldiers fighting with short weapons used blades. Based on the blades' basic movements of splitting and chopping, blade practitioners have come up with numerous sets of blade techniques which have been coordinated with various footwork and steps to form routines. Current schools of blade techniques include *Tai Chi* Blade, *Mei Hua* (plum blossom) Blade, *Ba Gua* Blade, *Ba Men Jin Suo* (eight doors with gold locks) Blade, *Ri Yue Qian Kun* (the sun, moon, heaven and earth) Blade and *Shaolin Shuang Dao Shi Ba Gun* (*Shaolin* double blades with eighteen rolling techniques).

武术
Chinese Martial Arts

太极刀

太极刀又称"太极十三刀"，是太极拳运动系列的短器械。太极刀法将太极拳与刀法融会贯通，把各种刀法和步法、手法巧妙地编排起来，既不失太极拳的风格，又给人一种刀法多变、劲力到位、身法自然的感觉。整个套路动作变化灵活、刚柔兼备，具有健身价值和观赏价值。

Tai Chi Dao

Tai Chi Dao, also known as *Tai Chi Shi San Dao* (*Shi San* means thirteen in Chinese), is the short weapon used in *Tai Chi Quan*. *Tai Chi Dao* techniques combine *Tai Chi Quan* with blade techniques, and integrate various sword techniques, hand movements and steps in a smart way that preserve the style of *Tai Chi Quan* while manifesting diversified sword techniques, in-place strength and natural body movements. With routines of flexible and changing movements and soft and tough traits, *Tai Chi Dao* boasts the double value of body-building and appreciation.

刀的历史

刀的历史悠久，在商周时期（前1600—前256年）青铜刀就很普及，但青铜刀质地脆，缺少韧性，没有正式用于格斗。秦汉时期，刀的制作工艺得到极大发展，出现用于实战的战刀。战场上主要的短兵器是环首刀，诞生于汉代，是一种柄呈环形的铁质长刀，一侧开刃，另一侧是厚实的刀脊，质地坚韧，威力很大。这一时期还出现了样式精美、做工精良的佩刀，是身份、地位、等级的象征。三国时期，短柄环首刀已成为军队中普遍装备的格斗器械；长柄大刀也不断发展，但未在军中普及。

隋唐时期，刀的炼铸技艺更加先进，炼出的刀更加坚韧锋利。普遍使用的刀主要有横刀和陌刀。横刀是军队士兵普遍装备的战斗用佩刀；陌刀是步兵使用的双刃长刀。到了宋代，刀的形制发生了变化，刀的种类逐渐增多，据《武经总要》记载，当

• 环首刀

Huan Shou Dao (a blade with a ring at the end of the blade handle)

- 短柄翘首铜刀（商）
Short-hilt *Qiao Shou* (Raised Head) Bronze Blade
(Shang Dynasty, 1600 B.C.-1046 B.C.)

- 缠丝线把鱼皮鞘铁腰刀(清)
Iron Broadsword with Fish-skin Scabbard and Silk-
thread-twined Handle (Qing Dynasty, 1644-1911)

时的刀主要有手刀、掉刀、屈刀、偃月刀、戟刀、眉尖刀、凤嘴刀、笔刀等。其中
只有手刀是短柄的，其余七种都是装有长柄的。手刀柄短，可以单手握执，刀身较
宽，前锐后平，刀头微微上翘，有护手。在手刀的基础上出现了多种长柄刀。

元明时期，海外交往比较频繁，波斯刀、日本倭刀传入中国，对中国造刀形制
和工艺的影响很大。刀是明代步兵、骑兵必备的兵器，主要形制有长刀、短刀、腰
刀三种。长刀仿日本刀式，刀身和刀柄较长，双手握柄。短刀刀身较弯，是骑兵所
用。腰刀佩戴在腰间，与藤牌合用。清代的军刀制式有顺刀、窝刀、札刀、朴刀、
斩马刀等。皇室佩刀装具非常华丽，刀上镂金，镶嵌珠宝，刀鞘包裹鱼皮，刀套镂
花，近刀鞘口一段有铜鼓，用来拴刀带。民间的刀型更是丰富，单刀有腰刀、砍
刀、柳叶刀、雁翎刀、大环刀等，双刀有鸳鸯刀、蝴蝶刀等。

History of Blade

The blade has a time-honored history which can be traced back to the Shang and Zhou Dynasties (1600 B.C.-256 B.C.), when bronze swords were already in wide use except for official use in combat due to its brittleness and lack of flexibility. In the Qin and Han Dynasties (221 B.C.–220 A.D.), sword manufacutring techniques witnessed much progress and there appeared blades for actual combat. *Huan Shou Dao* (a blade with a ring at the end of the blade handle), a major weapon in the battlefield that came into being in the Han Dynasty (206 B.C.–220 A.D.), is a long iron sword whose hilt is in the shape of a ring with cutting edge on one side and thick fuller on the other. This blade is of strong texture and great strength. During this period, there also emerged the exquisite and refined walking saber, a symble of identity, social status and hierarchic rank. By the Three Kingdoms Period (220-280), short-hilt *Huan Shou Dao* had become a common combat weapon through the army, accompanied by the development of long-hilt big blades that were not in common use in the army.

In the Sui and Tang Dynasties (581-907), sword casting technologies were even more advanced so swords with sharper edges and stronger texture were produced. Blades commonly used were *Heng Dao* (horizontal blade) and *Mo Dao*, the former being a common combat-use walking saber for soldiers and the latter being a double-edged long saber for infantrymen. In the Song Dynasty (960-1279), the blade took different forms and embraced more categories. According to the record in *Wu Jing Zong Yao* (*Collection of the Most Important Military Techniques*), a Chinese military compendium, the blade in the Song Dynasty was mainly divided into *Shou Dao* (handheld knife), *Diao Dao* (a blade with a wide body and long handle), *Qu Dao* (a blade with a slanting and long body and long handle), *Yan Yue Dao* (crescent-shaped blade), *Ji Dao* (a knife with a straight blade and crescent-shaped blade on one side), *Mei Jian Dao* (eyebrow knife), *Feng Zui Dao* (phenix-beak-shaped blade)and *Bi Dao* (brush-like blade), of which only *Shou Dao* had a short hilt. *Shou Dao* can be handled with a single hand; it has a broad blade that is sharp in the front and flat in the back;

• 清代士兵像

Portrait of the Soldier in the Qing Dynasty (1644-1911)

its pommel turns slightly upward; and it is equipped with a guard. Based on *Shou Dao*, many long-hilt blades have been developed.

In the Yuan and Ming Dynasties (1279-1644), due to the frequent foreign exchanges, Persian sword and Japanese swords found their way into China and posed great influences on China's sword forms and manufacturing techniques. The blade is a requisite weapon for infantry and cavalry in the Ming Dynasty (1368-1644) in three major forms of long blade, short blade and waist blade. Long blade imitates the Japanese blade and has a relatively long blade body and hilt, and needs both hands to handle. Short blade has a narrow blade body and is for cavalry use. Waist blade is worn at the waist with a cane shield. In the Qing Dynasty (1644-1911), a military blade or saber is divided into *Shun Dao* (half-sword-like blade), *Wo Dao, Zha Dao, Pu Dao* and *Zhan Ma Dao* (horse-beheaded blade). Royal walking sword is magnificent and gilded with gold and jewelry decorations. The scabbard is wrapped with fish skin, the case engraved with flowers and a copper drum near the locket to tie the sword belt. Blade used by the general public manifested even more forms, with single blade like broadsword, hacking knife, lancet, *Yan Ling Dao* (goose plume blade) and long-hilt broadsword with rings, and double blade like Lovers Blades and Butterfly Blades.

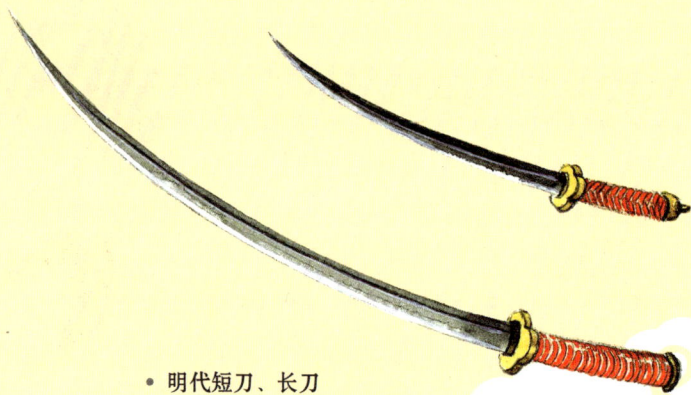

• 明代短刀、长刀
Short and Long Blades in the Ming Dynasty (1368-1644)

《三国演义》

　　《三国演义》是中国第一部长篇章回体历史演义小说，作者罗贯中（约1330年—约1400年）。小说描写了三国时期以曹操、刘备、孙权为首的三个政治、军事集团之间的矛盾和斗争，展示了那个时代尖锐复杂又极具特色的政治军事冲突，对后世影响深远。三国时期群雄逐鹿，征伐不断，各种谋略战法的应用达到高峰，而武器装备更是名目繁多，各显神通，在战场上扮演着重要角色。小说对名将的兵器进行了重点描写和艺术加工，如关羽的青龙偃月刀、张飞的丈八点钢矛、吕布的方天画戟等。

Romance of the Three Kingdoms

Romance of the Three Kingdoms is China's first historical serial novel in chapters with couplet titles written by Luo Guanzhong (about 1330-1400). Through the description of the conflict and fight between the three political and military blocs led by Cao Cao, Liu Bei and Sun Quan, this novel presents the complicated and sharp political and military conflicts unique

• 偃月刀

　　在中国著名的古典小说《三国演义》中，有许多关于古代军事战争场面以及兵器使用的细致描写。例如，蜀国大将关羽（？—220）骁勇善战，义重如山，被后人尊称为"武圣"。他所用的刀，刀身狭长，形如弯月，刀身上有青龙图案，又称"青龙偃月刀"，刀头有钩，刀背有突出锯齿利刃，又称"冷艳锯"。

Yan Yue Dao

In *Romance of the Three Kindoms*, one of the Four Great Classical Novels of Chinese literature, there are detailed descriptions on ancient military war scenes and application of weapons. For example, Guan Yu (?-220), a general in the state of Shu, is battlewise, loyal and righteous. He is honored as the "Saint of War" by later generations. The blade he used features a narrow, long and crescent-shaped body carved with black dragon patterns, hence its name *Qing Long Yan Yue Dao* (Black-dragon crescent-shaped blade). There is a hook at the point and jagged edges at the fuller, hence its another name *Leng Yan Ju* (icy and elegant saw).

to that era and influential in later generations. During the Three Kingdoms Period (220-280), feudal lords rivaled and fought with one another and applied strategies and tactics in a way unimaginable to predecessors. Moreover, countless weapons played an important role in the battlefield in this period with their distinct advantages. The novel mainly portrays weapons of famous generals in an artistic way, such as *Qing Long Yan Yue Dao* (Black-dragon crescent-shaped blade) of Guan Yu, *Zhang Ba Dian Gang Mao* (eight-*zhang* steel-pointing lance, 1 *zhang* is about 3.33 meters) of Zhang Fei and *Fang Tian Hua* Ji (a halberd with colored patterns and "井" shaped top) of Lü Bu.

• 《关羽擒将图》商喜（明）

《关羽擒将图》取材于三国时期的蜀汉大将关羽水淹七军、生擒庞德的故事。画中的关羽头包蓝巾、身穿绿袍，卧蚕眉，丹凤眼，长髯在胸前飘拂，气宇轩昂地端坐在山石之上。左有拔剑叱喝的义子关平，右有手捧青龙偃月刀的猛将周仓。绑在石柱上的庞德神情坚毅，誓死不降。

Picture of Guan Yu Capturing Pang De By Shang Xi (Ming Dynasty, 1368-1644)

This painting is based on the story that Guan Yu flooded the seven armies and captured the general Pang De. In this painting, Guan Yu is sitting in dignity on a mountain rock in a blue kerchief and green robe with bushy eyebrows, phoenix eyes and a long beard fleeting in front of his chest. To his left stands Guan Ping, his adopted son, who is taking out the sword and shouting at Pang De. To his right stands the brave Zhou Cang, who is holding the *Qing Long Yan Yue Dao* (Black-dragon crescent-shaped blade). Pang De is tied to the stone column and looks resolute as if he would rather die than surrender.

《水浒传》里的两把宝刀

在古典小说《水浒传》里，梁山好汉们使用的短兵器多为刀，小说中浓墨重彩地描写了两把宝刀。一把是林冲买的龙吟宝刀。林冲绰号豹子头，东京（今河南开封）八十万禁军教头，生性耿直，武艺高强，在街上见到有人卖刀，"清光夺目,冷气侵人。远看如玉沼春冰,近看似琼台瑞雪。花纹密布……"所谓"鲜花赠美人，宝刀配英雄"，林冲不惜重金买下宝刀，还彻夜不眠不休地舞刀，可见林冲爱刀、识刀、惜刀。另一把是杨志卖的家传宝刀。杨志是北宋时期杨家将的后代，绰号"青面兽"。因渎职得罪了上司，身无分文，走投无路，只好卖掉祖传宝刀。这把刀有三大特色，一是砍铜剁铁，刀口不卷；二是吹毛得过；三是杀人刀上不沾血。

Two Precious Blades in *Outlaws of the Marsh*

In the classic novel of the *Outlaws of the Marsh*, most short weapons used by the 108 outlaws on Mount Liang are blades. In particular, this novel depicts two precious blades in detail, one of which is the blade bought by Lin Chong, known as *Long Yin Bao Dao* (dragon-crooning

· 《水浒传》版画
Print of *Outlaws of the Marsh*

treasure blade) in Chinese. Lin Chong, nicknamed "Panther Head", was an arms instructor of the 800,000 mighty imperial guards in Dongjing (today's Kaifeng in Henan Province). He was an honest and straightforward man excelling in martial arts. One day in the street, he saw someone selling a blade with an "excellent blade that delivered chilly and dazzling shines. Looking from afar, it resembled the spring ice in a jade-like pond; looked hard by, it is like the auspicious snow covering a jeweled tower. Being densely patterned..." As the old saying goes, "Flowers are a match for beauty and precious blades are a match for heroes." Lin Chong bought the blade despite the high price and would lay awake all day long to practice martial arts techniques with it, which demonstrated his love, appreciation and cherishing of the blade. The other one elaborated in the novel is the ancestral blade put on sale by Yang Zhi. Yang Zhi, nicknamed "Blue-Faced Beast", was a descendent of generals, the grandson of the Duke Yang Linggong in the Northern Song Dynasty (960-1127). He enraged his senior officials due to misconduct and was left with no money. Therefore, he had to sell the ancestral blade. The rare blade boasted three features: first, it can cut copper and pierce iron without curling the edge; second, it can cut a hair blown against it; third, it can kill a man and come away clean.

> 枪

　　枪由古代兵器矛发展而来，长而锋利，杀伤力强，使用灵便，精微独到，有"百兵之王"之称。枪的式样繁多、用途各异，广泛用于步兵和骑兵。

> Spear

Spear developed from lance, an ancient weapon. It is long and sharp, highly lethal, convenient to utilize, tricky and unique, and known as the "king of all weapons". Spears have various types and different functions and were widely used by infantries and cavalries.

矛

　　矛是用于直刺、扎挑的长兵器，由尖利的矛头和矛柄组成。早期战车上配备有矛，作为进攻兵器，大规模兴起于汉末。矛比较长，通常为两米左右，有的竟可以达四米多。矛用于骑兵作战曾经很有效，但是由于很长，不经过严格训练不容易掌握，以后开始向枪转变。

Lance

Lance is a long weapon for direct stab and prick, consisting of sharp lancehead and handgrip. Early chariots were equipped with lances as offensive weapons. Large-scale use of lance appeared in the end of the Han Dynasty (206 B.C.- 220 A.D.). Lance is relatively long, usually with a length of two meters and some were even as long as over four meters. Lance used to be quite effective in cavalry fighting, but due to its length, it was difficult to master without strict training. Therefore, lance is gradually transformed into spear.

吴王夫差使用的青铜矛头

1983年，在湖北江陵马山5号墓中出土了吴王夫差（？—前473年）自用青铜矛，全长29.5厘米，宽5.5厘米。矛身中线起脊，两面脊上均有血槽，血槽后端各铸一兽首形鼻纽。骹口（用来装柄的部位）扁圆中空。此矛铸造精湛，周身满饰菱形暗纹。

Head of Bronze Lance Used by King Fu Chai of Wu

A bronze lance used by King Fu Chai of Wu (?-473 B.C.) was unearthed from Mashan No. 5 Tomb in Jiangling, Hubei Province in 1983. The lance is 29.5 centimeters long and 5.5 centimeters wide. In the middle of the lance body is the lance ridge, with blood grooves on its both sides. At the end of both grooves are two beast-head-shaped *Bi Niu* (nose-shaped knot). The *Jiao Kou* (space for the handgrip) is flat and round in shape and hollow inside. The lance is delicately cast and the surface is full of diamond-shaped geometric dark patterns.

蛇矛

蛇矛是矛的一种，两面有刃，刃部扁平，矛尖弯曲如蛇。

Snake Lance

Snake lance is one type of lance. It has blades on both sides. The blades are flat and the lancehead is curving like a snake.

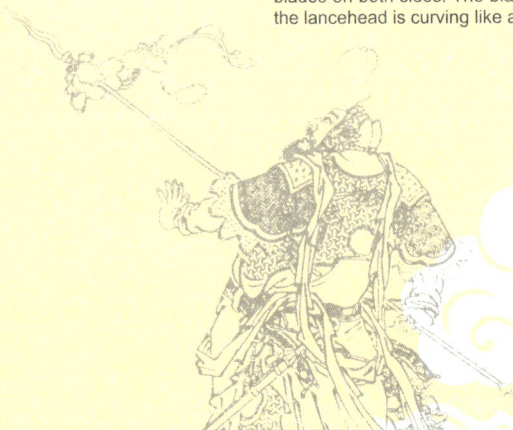

枪由枪尖、枪缨、枪杆组成，枪尖以铜、铁制成，头尖、脊高、刃薄。枪缨是枪头下面的装饰物，古时多用马鬃或牛尾，现在多用细麻丝制成。作战时，抖动枪缨可以迷乱对方的视线，平时演练可壮声势。枪杆古时多用木制，直而不曲。枪有长枪、短枪之别，又有单枪、双枪之分。

枪法种类繁多，但都以灵动快捷的招法见长，练枪时，身法灵活多变，步法轻灵快速，用枪者往往自己也会因此增加潇洒灵动之气。枪术可以单练，也可与其他武器对练，如刀对枪、剑对枪等。

A spear consists of the spear tip, spear tassel and spear stem. The spear tip is made of bronze and iron with sharp head, high ridge and thin blade. The spear tassel is the decoration under the spearhead and was usually made from horsehair or cow tail in ancient times. Now it is often made from thin hemp thread. Shaking the spear tassel can obfuscate the enemy's eyesight during fighting and enhance practitioners' enthusiasm in daily trainings. The spear stem was often made of wood in ancient times, which was very straight. Spears have different types, including long spear, short spear, or single spear and double spear.

枪头
Spearhead

枪缨
Spear Tassel

枪杆
Spear Stem

● **枪的结构示意图**
Spear Structure

● 枪头（宋）
Spearhead (Song Dynasty, 960-1279)

There are various spear techniques, but all are featured with flexible and agile moves. While practicing spear, the spear user should have flexible and changeful body movements and light and agile footwork, which usually add elegance to the spear user him/herself. Spear techniques can be practiced by oneself or counter practiced with other weapons, such as broadsword vs. spear, sword vs. spear, etc.

少林枪法

少林枪法是在少林棍法的基础上，吸收各派枪法的精华，经过融会贯通而创。少林枪法以枪为主，兼用棍法，枪棍合一，刚柔兼济。少林枪法系统合理，精妙实用，所以受到武林人士的珍视，传播范围很广。

Shaolin Spear Techniques

Shaolin spear techniques were created based on *Shaolin* staff techniques, absorbing the essence of different schools of spear techniques and achieving perfection through comprehensive study of them. *Shaolin* spear techniques focus on the spear with staff techniques as supplement, combining the two and attaching equal importance to toughness and softness. *Shaolin* spear techniques are scientific, exquisite and practical, thus cherished by martial artists and spread widely.

● 刀枪对练的少林武僧 （图片提供：FOTOE）
Shaolin Monks Are Counter-practicing with Broadsword and Spear.

峨嵋枪法

峨嵋枪法在古代枪法中占有重要地位，其历史悠久，由四川峨嵋山普恩禅师始创。峨眉枪法功架优美、劲力饱满、步活身灵、变化多端，"枪似游龙扎一点，舞动生花妙无穷"。峨嵋的枪法理论体系较为完备，强调意、气、力、技的综合发挥，并提出了宜静、宜动、攻守、审势等技击战略战术法则和枪法要诀。

Emei Spear Techniques

Emei spear techniques played an important role in ancient spear techniques. It has a long history, created by Chan Master Pu En of *Emei* Mountain in Sichuan Province. *Emei* spear techniques are featured with elegant gestures, strong physical strength, flexible movements of feet and body and various changes. "The spear is just like a dancing dragon, creating infinite wonders from one point." The theoretical system of *Emei* spear techniques is relatively complete, emphasizing the comprehensive play of will, spirit, physical strength and skills. It also presents strategic offensive tactics and principles and the essence of *Emei* spear techniques related to stillness and movement, offense and defense and assessment of the situation.

枪的历史

晋代开始逐渐流行用枪，唐代以后矛多称"枪"，唐代之后善枪的人很多。《五代史·王彦章传》记载："彦章持一铁枪，骑而驰突，奋疾如飞，而他人莫能举也，军中号王铁枪。"可见马上用枪已经出现在军中。宋代，枪的发展最为繁盛，有长枪、钩镰枪、九曲枪、梨花枪、笔枪、雁翎枪、绿沉枪、浑铁枪、龙头枪、龙刀枪、虎牙枪、虎头枪等。宋代军队配备的长兵器以枪为主，步兵、骑兵都要操练枪法。到了明清，火器大规模运用，受此影响，枪在战争中的作用有所减弱，但仍然是军队中最常用的冷兵器。

History of Spear

Spears became popular during the Jin Dynasty (265-420). Lances were usually called "spears" since the Tang Dynasty (618-907), from when many people were good at using spears. According to the record in *History of Five Dynasties • Biography of Wang Yanzhang*, "Yanzhang held an iron spear and rode a horse, rushing forward as if on wings. No one could defeat him and he was called Wang Tieqiang (iron spear) in the military." It showed that there had already been spear practicing on the horseback in the military. The development of spears boosted during the Song Dynasty (960-1279), with the appearance of long spear, *Gou Lian* (sickle-shaped) spear, *Jiu Qu* spear, *Li Hua* (pear blossom) spear, *Bi* (brush-pen-shaped) spear, *Yan Ling* spear, *Lu Chen* spear (made of *Lu Chen*, a type of bamboo), *Hun Tie* spear, *Long Tou* (dragon head) spear, *Long Dao* spear (with sword at the spearhead), *Hu Ya* (tiger-teeth) spear, *Hu Tou* (tiger-head) spear, etc. During the Song Dynasty, long weapons equipped for the military were mainly spears and both infantries and cavalries must practice spear techniques. Firearms began to be used at a large scale in the Ming Dynasty (1368-1644); therefore, spears' importance in wars were reduced, but still remained the most commonly used cold weapon in the military.

• 古代骑兵作战的场面
War Scene of Ancient Cavalries

宋代用枪名将

宋代涌现出许多善用枪的名将。宋代李全之妻杨妙贞所创梨花枪套路，世称"二十年梨花枪，天下无敌手"。梨花枪比较特别，是长枪和火器的结合兵器，用长枪缚一喷火筒，用火药烧灼而杀伤敌人，也可用枪头刺杀。抗辽的杨家将一家祖孙三代都骁勇善战，立下了赫赫战功。杨家众将都擅长使用长枪，家传枪法变化无穷，所向无敌，世称"杨家枪"。宋代抗金将领岳飞，是中国历史上著名的战略家、军事家。其率领的军队被称为"岳家军"，历史上有"撼山易，撼岳家军难"之说。岳飞性格刚毅勇敢，骁勇善战，武功精湛，技艺出众，战功卓著。岳飞善使铁枪，岳家枪技击方法独特，号称"枪中之王"。岳家枪动作古朴，招招制敌，一击必杀，进攻有刺、戳、点、扫、挑；防守有格、拨、架、挡、滒。它的独特之处是将防守和进攻融为一体，攻防一次完成；防中带攻，攻中设防，使敌人无还击之机。

• 岳飞画像
Portrait of Yue Fei

武
术

Chinese Martial Arts

Famous Spear Warriors in the Song Dynasty (960-1279)

The Song Dynasty saw the emerging of many warriors good at using spear. Yang Miaozhen, wife of Li Quan in the Song Dynasty, created the techniques of *Li Hua* spear, which was called "twenty-year-old techniques with no rival in the world". *Li Hua* spear was a rather special weapon for combining the functions of long spears and firearms. With a fire-spraying tube tied on the long spear, it can burn the enemy with gunpowder and stab with the spearhead. The three generations of the Yang family who fought against Liao were all brave and good at fighting and achieved marvelous battlefield success. The Yang warriors were all skilled in long spears and their hereditary spear techniques were changeful and invincible, honored as the "spear techniques of the Yang family" by the world. Yue Fei, general in the war against Jin in the Song Dynasty, was a famous strategist and in Chinese history. The army led by him was called "Yue Army". There was a saying goes like this in the history, "To defeat Yue Army is even harder than to move a mountain." Yue Fei was resolute, courageous, expert at fighting and had exquisite martial art skills, distinguished techniques and outstanding battlefield achievements. He was good at iron spear. The spear techniques of Yue were unique in the art of attack and defense and were called "King of Spear Techniques". They were featured with simple but deadly moves and one move could kill the rival. Offensive moves included stabbing, poking, clicking, sweeping and picking, and defensive moves, confining, pushing, framing, fending and trickling. The uniqueness is the combination of offense and defense and the completion of the two in one strike. Such inseparable mix of offense and defense allowed no chance for the rival to fight back.

> 剑

　　剑属双刃短兵器，运用起来的特点是刚柔相济、优美自如，飘洒轻快，有"百刃之君"之美称。

　　剑由剑身、剑柄组成，剑身由剑锋、剑刃、剑尖、剑脊组成。剑柄由剑首、剑柄、剑格组成。剑有

> Sword

Sword belongs to double-edged short weapon and features of its practice are combing toughness and softness, elegant, free, graceful and lively. It is honored the Gentleman of Blades.

A sword consists of the body and stem. The body is made up of edge, blade, tip and ridge, and the stem, head, handgrip and *Jian Ge* (a protruding part that protects the hand holding the sword).

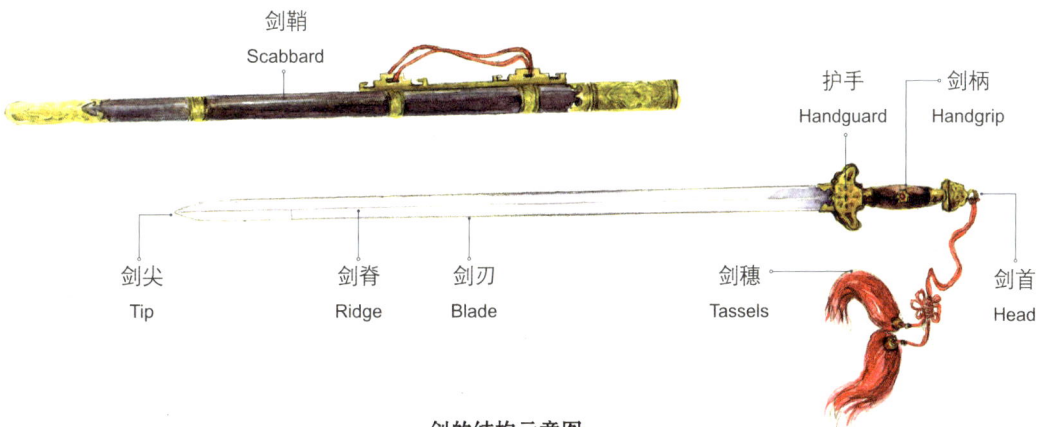

剑鞘
Scabbard

护手
Handguard

剑柄
Handgrip

剑尖
Tip

剑脊
Ridge

剑刃
Blade

剑穗
Tassels

剑首
Head

• 剑的结构示意图
Sword Structure

长剑、短剑、大剑、穗剑、单剑、双剑之分。

剑有挂、刺、点、撩、挑、提、截、扫、格等技法。剑术的动作要求轻快敏捷，如行云流水，有"剑如飞风"之说。剑术套路很多，主要有太极剑、武当剑、峨眉剑、昆仑剑、青龙剑、八仙剑、七星剑等。

Swords have various types including long sword, short sword, big sword, sword with tassels, single sword and double sword.

Sword techniques include hanging, stabbing, clicking, holding up, picking, lifting, cutting, sweeping, confining, etc. The movement of sword techniques should be light and agile like floating clouds and flowing water, thus being called "Sword flies like wind". Sword techniques have various tricks, mainly including *Tai Chi* sword, *Wudang* sword, *Emei* sword, *Kunlun* sword, *Qing Long* (black dragon) sword, *Ba Xian* (The Eight Immortals) sword, *Qi Xing* (seven-star) sword, etc.

太极剑

太极剑是在剑术的基础上吸收太极拳的精髓发展而成的，兼有太极拳与剑术的特点。一方面太极剑像太极拳一样，表现出绵柔不断、轻灵柔和、用意不用力的特点，另一方面还要表现出优美潇洒的身法、清楚的剑法、形神兼备的剑术演练风格。太极剑的动作要求以意导剑，剑身合一。剑法讲求多变，避实击虚。以腰力带动剑的动作，劲透剑身。技击时要手空剑活，剑法灵巧，剑圈宜先大后小，弧圈相连。

太极剑集健身、技击、表演于一体，是非常有益的运动。长期练习，可以提高神经系统的机能，延缓大脑的衰老，使全身气血流畅，呼吸系统得到改善。还可以锻炼身体的各个部位，提高肌肉韧性。除了强身健体，练习太极剑还能调养精神状态，达到生理和心理的平衡。

Tai Chi Sword

Tai Chi sword was developed on the base of sword techniques and by absorbing the essence of *Tai Chi Quan*, embodying the features of the both. On the one hand, *Tai Chi* sword is as soft and light as *Tai Chi Quan*, continuously deploying the will power instead of physical power. On the other hand, *Tai Chi* sword shows beautiful and elegant body gestures and clear sword skills just as sword techniques do, creating the unify of form and spirit. *Tai Chi* sword moves require guiding the sword with mind and combining sword with the practitioner's body. Sword techniques focus on changes and avoiding substance to attack emptiness. Strength from the waist drives the movement of the sword and such strength should saturate the sword. In offense and defense, one's hands, the sword and techniques should all be flexible and the circles drawn by the sword had better be from big to small in a continuous way.

   Tai Chi sword combines physical exercise, attack techniques and performance, thus a very beneficial sports event. Long-term practice of *Tai Chi* sword can help improve functions of the nerve system, delay brain aging, smooth the flow of blood and better the respiratory system. It can also exercise every part of the body and enhance muscle tenacity. In addition to body building, *Tai Chi* sword can nurse the mental state to reach a balance between physiology and psychology.

• 练习太极剑的老人
An Old Man is Practicing *Tai Chi* Sword

剑的历史

剑脱胎于矛形兵器及短匕首，春秋战国时期，斗剑、佩剑之风盛行。王侯贵族有着豢养剑士、观击剑的嗜好，击剑成为专门的活动。赵惠文王（公元前298—公元前266在位）养了三千多名剑客，观看击剑成瘾。剑术的好坏都关系到格斗者的生死存亡，所以剑术逐渐发展成为一项实战技能，出现了专门的剑术家，以及论述剑术的著作。《剑技》中以"持短入长，倏忽纵横"概括了击剑的特点。《庄子·说剑》中以"十步一人，千里不留行"来形容剑术的超绝。

春秋晚期至战国中期是铜剑发展的高峰期，青铜铸造业发达，铸剑技艺高超，制剑数量极大。南方的吴越地区多丘陵丛林，水网纵横，军队作战以水兵为主，配备剑、盾等兵器，对剑的重视，极大地促进了剑术和铸剑技术的发展。吴王夫差、越王勾践等称雄一时的霸主皆配有宝剑。古代传说中的名剑，如干将、莫邪、龙泉、太阿、纯钧、湛卢、鱼肠、巨阙等，相传也冶铸于这一时期。关于它们的铸造，留下了许多动人的故事。

秦汉时期，剑术已很精备，击剑显示了武艺造诣的深浅。剑不但是布兵、骑兵的重要武器，名士、侠客们仗剑远游也成为风尚。秦汉时期还颁布有法令，对官吏佩剑有明确的要求，以此来代表权力的威严。

隋唐五代时期，短兵器以刀为主，剑已经失去了实战价值，成为民间习武器械，并开始有了娱乐化的表现。剑术一直是深受人们喜爱的武术项目，佩剑之风仍很盛行。在举行宴饮时，舞剑助兴成为一种社会风气。击剑之风逐渐被剑舞所取代。唐代的剑术已很高超、成熟，精通剑术的人很多。裴旻的剑术独冠一时，剑在他的手里，仿佛有了生命，他的剑术与李白（701–762）的诗歌、张旭的草书并称"唐代三

• 铜剑(春秋)
Bronze Sword (Spring and Autumn Period, 770 B.C.-476 B.C.)

- 兽首短剑(春秋)

Short Sword with a Beast-head-shaped Decoration (Spring and Autumn Period, 770 B.C.-476 B.C.)

- 越王勾践剑

勾践是春秋末期越国的君主。在夫椒山（今江苏吴县西南）的吴越战争中，越兵大败。勾践为了保存力量，采用谋士范蠡的计谋，向吴称臣乞和。勾践归国后，不忘灭吴雪耻，卧薪尝胆（勾践睡觉睡在柴草上，吃饭睡觉前都尝一尝苦胆，励精图治以图复国。后演变为成语，形容人刻苦自励），休养生息，富国强兵。后来勾践举兵伐吴，灭了吴国。越王勾践剑通高55.7厘米，宽4.6厘米，柄长8.4厘米，重875克。剑首外翻卷成圆箍形，剑身中脊起棱，布满黑色菱形暗格花纹，剑格正面镶有蓝色琉璃，背面镶有绿松石。靠近剑格的地方有两行八字鸟篆铭文："越王鸠浅（勾践），自乍（作）用剑"。此剑在1965年出土于湖北省荆州市市望山楚墓，出土时，宝剑虽然已在地下埋藏了两千多年，仍锋利无比，20多层的复印纸一划即破。

Sword of the King Gou Jian of Yue

Gou Jian was the King of the State of Yue during late Spring and Autumn Period (770 B.C.-476 B.C.). The Yue army was totally defeated in the Wu-Yue war in Fujiao Mountain (southwest of today's Wu County in Jiangsu Province). To reserve strength, Gou Jian took the advice from his advisor Fan Li, giving up fighting and begging for peace from Wu. Gou Jian always kept destroying Wu in mind to wipe out the humiliation that Yue suffered. He exercised *Wo Xin Chang Dan* (Gou Jian slept on firewood and tasted gall before eating and sleeping. He made every effort to rejuvenate Yue. Such practice gradually became an idiom later, indicating that one is extremely hard-working and self-motivated.), reduced people's burden and focused on economic development and army building domestically. Later on, Gou Jian led his army to attack Wu and defeated it. His sword is 55.7 cm long with an 8.4-cm-long stem, 4.6 cm wide and 875 gram weight. The sword head rolled outwards to form a hoop. Covered by black diamond-shaped dark patterns, the body had a ridge from its middle part. The *Jian Ge* was decorated by blue glaze on the front side and kallaite on the back. Near the *Jian Ge* were eight Chinese characters in *Niao Zhuan* (a type of seal characters that looked like the prints of bird paws) in two lines, "Sword of King Jiu Qian (Gou Jian) of Wu, made and used by himself." This sword was unearthed in 1965 in Chu Tomb, Shiwang Mountain of Jingzhou, Hubei Province. Being buried under earth for over 2,000 years, the precious sword was still extremely sharp when unearthed, piercing through more than 20 layers of copy paper with just one scratch.

绝"。唐开元年间（713-741）的公孙大娘，以善舞剑器而闻名于世。据说，书法家张旭因观看了公孙大娘的剑舞，而深受启发，书法大为长进。

从宋代一直到清代，在军队中，剑一般只作为权利、身份的象征。但在民间，剑被广泛使用，成为习武之人最常使用的兵器之一。

纵观剑的发展历史，剑不仅可作为格斗、防身、练武的器械，还具有其他用途，如作为身份、地位、等级的象征，作为佛教、道教的法器，作为文人士大夫的风雅佩饰。

History of Sword

The sword evolved from lance-shaped weapons and short daggers. During the Spring and Autumn Period and the Warring States Period (770 B.C.-221 B.C.), sword contest and sword wearing were very popular. People from noble and royal families had the hobby of feeding swordsmen and viewing sword contests, and fencing became a specialized activity. King Huiwen of Zhao (on the throne from 298 B.C.-266 B.C.) fed over 3,000 swordsmen and was obsessed with watching sword contests. The level of swordsmanship bore on the contestant's chance of survival; therefore, swordsmanship gradually turned into a practical skill and professional swordsmen and swordsmanship works began to emerge. Swordsmanship summarized the features of practicing sword as "reaching far with short-range moves in a swift and free manner". *Chuang Tzu•On Sword* described the extraordinary brilliance of swordsmanship as "The swordsman can kill the enemy swiftly within every ten steps and then immediately go to somewhere several thousand miles away where nobody can find him."

The period between late Spring and Autumn Period (770 B.C.-476 B.C.) and the middle of the Warring States Period (475 B.C.-221 B.C.) saw the boost of bronze swords with advanced bronze foundry industry, excellent foundry technologies and a large amount of finished swords. The Wu and Yue regions (mainly refer to today's Jiangsu and Zhejiang Provinces) in south China had many hills and jungles and interwoven water channels. Marines were the major fighting force in the military, equipped with sword, shield and other weapons. The great importance attached to sword significantly promoted the development of swordsmanship and foundry technologies. King Fu Chai of Wu, King Gou Jian of Yue and other Kings who once ruled the roost all wore precious swords. Legendary famous swords, such as *Ganjiang, Moye, Longquan, Tai'e, Chunjun, Zhanlu, Yuchang and Juque,* were said to be cast during this period. Many moving stories about the foundry of these swords have been passed down through the history.

Swordsmanship had been very mature during the Qin and Han dynasties (221 B.C.-220 A.D.). It reflected one's level of martial art skills. Swords were important weapons for infantries and cavalries, and celebrities and swordsmen followed the fashion of wearing swords and traveling far. During this period, regulations were issued to set clear requirements on how officials should wear swords to embody the majesty of power.

During the Sui and Tang Dynasties and the Five Dynasties (581-960), the blade played the dominating role among short weapons. Swords had lost actual-combat values and became a weapon of martial art practice for common people, starting to show the entertaining function. Swordsmanship had been a favorite martial arts event for people and the wearing of swords was still in fashion. Performing sword dance to create merrier atmosphere in feasts was a social custom and gradually sword contest was replaced by sword dance. Swordsmanship had been excellent and mature and many people had mastered the essence of swordsmanship during the Tang Dynasty (618-907). Pei Min took the lead in swordsmanship because swords in his hand were alive. His swordsmanship, Li Bai's (701-762) poem and Zhang Xu's cursive were collectively called Three Wonders of the Tang Dynasty. Aunt Gongsun, living in the Kaiyuan period of the Tang Dynasty (713-741), was well-known for her excellent sword dance. Legend says that calligrapher Zhang Xu was greatly inspired by Aunt Gongsun's sword dance and made huge progress in calligraphy.

From the Song Dynasty (960-1279) to the Qing Dynasty (1644-1911), sword was only regarded as a symbol of authority and identity in the military. But among common people, sword was widely used and became one of the favorite weapons for martial artists.

Reviewing its development history, sword has served as a tool for fighting, self-defense and martial arts practice. It also has many other functions: embodiment of one's identity, social status and official rank, appliance in Buddhism and Taoism, and elegant decoration of scholars and bureaucrats.

> 棍

棍是无刃长兵器，有"百兵之首"之称。棍取材简单，使用便利，是宜守宜攻的有力兵器，棍适合近战搏斗，比刀、枪的攻击范围大，有"枪扎一条线，棍扫一大片"的说法。棍在军事训练和武术练习中发挥着重要的作用。

棍的结构简单，是人类较早掌握的工具，原始社会的狩猎和战争中，人们就会利用棍来击打目标。随着棍的加工不断精细，人们在棍上镶嵌石片，或是把一端削尖，在棍的基础上，演化出了枪、矛等兵器。

棍有长短粗细之分，种类很多，仅长棍就有大棍、齐眉棍、少林棍、盘花棍、金箍棍、水火棍、梢子棍等。棍有劈、扫、挑、戳、砸、点、翻等技法，棍术的动作特

> Staff

Staff is a long edgeless weapon, honored as the "Ancestor of all weapons". It is made of simple raw materials and convenient to utilize, powerful and suitable for both offense and defense. Staff is appropriate for short-range fighting and has a wider attack range than the broadsword and spear. It is said that "The attack range of a spear is a line but that of a staff, an area." Staff plays an important role in military training and martial arts practice.

With a simple structure, staff is an earlier weapon mastered by human beings. In the primitive society, people were able to use staffs to attack targets in hunting and wars. As the processing of staffs was getting more mature, people started to inlay stone slices in the staff, or sharpen one end of it. Therefore, the spear, lance and other weapons emerged

少林棍

为明代少林寺武僧习武所用，通体一般粗细。

Shaolin Staff

Cudgels of this style were exclusively used during the Ming Dynasty (1368-1644) by kung fu monks inside the *Shaolin* Temple. It had no variation in thickness from end to tip.

齐眉棍

棍竖立与人眉高度相齐，故名。

Qimei Staff

Because of its length this cudgel got the name of *Qimei*, meaning "up to the eyebrows of a man when standing on end".

盘花棍

棍身刻有花纹，故名。

Panhua Staff

It got its name *Panhua*, flowers from the pattern inscribed on its shaft.

金箍棒

金箍棒长八尺左右，梢和根处均套有铁箍或铜箍，故名。

Gold-banded Staff

Nearly three meters long, this gold-banded cudgel had iron or bronze hoops on its ends.

水火棍

棍上涂有象征火的红色，以及象征水的黑色，有秉直、刚正之意，多为古时差役使用。

Shuihuo Staffl

Because of the red and black paints on its body, the former meaning fire and the latter, water and when combined the two meant justice. This cudgel was used by government runners in ancient times.

白棓

棒的一种，因多用白木制成，故名。

While Staff

A sort of cudgels, named after the white wood they were made with.

点是刚劲勇猛、快速多变、运动范围大。

棍类还有一类软兵器，基本式样是为几节木棍或铁棍，以索链相连。这类兵器弯折自由，是有效的攻击性器械。在武术中常用的有双节棍、三节棍。

on the basis of staff.

Staffs have various types according to length and thickness. In the category of long staff only, there are Big staff, *Qi Mei* (eyebrow-level) staff, *Shaolin* staff, *Pan Hua* (pattern-twisted) staff, *Jingu* staff, *Shui Huo* (water and fire) staff, *Shaozi* staff (two staffs connected together by iron rings), etc. Staff techniques include splitting, sweeping, picking, poking, smashing, clicking, turning, etc. Staff moves are strong and powerful, swift and changeful, and have a wide moving scale.

Staffs also include soft weapons, the basic structure of which is that several wood or iron staffs are linked by chains. Such soft weapons can bend flexibly, thus a very effective offensive weapon. Double-section staff (Nunchaku) and three-section staff are commonly used in martial arts.

● 双节棍

由两根等长的短棍中间以铁链连接而成，短小精悍，可以折叠，使用方便，可以将双节棍叠在一起拿着使用，也可以拿着任何一端使用，威力很大。

Nunchaku

It is made up of two short sticks of equal length which are linked by an iron chain. It is short, forceful, foldable and convenient to use. One can fold the two sticks of the Nunchaku to fight or hold either stick. It is a very powerful weapon.

《中国红》出版编辑委员会

传统手工艺 Traditional Chinese Crafts	风筝 Kites	面具 Masks
中国色彩 Colorful China	盆景 Bonsai	鼻烟壶 Snuff Bottles
刺绣 Chinese Embroidery	景泰蓝 Cloisonné	颐和园 The Summer Palace
中国禅 Zen	泥塑 Clay Sculpture	丝绸之路 The Silk Road
棋艺 Art of Chesses	面塑 Dough Figuring	汉字 Chinese Characters
宋词 Ci-Poems of the Song Dynasty	大运河 Grand Canal	中国木偶艺术 Chinese Puppet Arts
茶马古道 Ancient Tea-Horse Road	历史名城 Historical Cities	古代兵书 Ancient Book on the Art of War
中国名湖 Famous Lakes in China	中国结 Chinese Knots	道教文化 Daoism Culture in China
中国料器 Chinese Glassware	兵马俑 Terracotta Army	古代交通 Ancient Traffic
帝王陵寝 Imperial Mausoleum	皮影 Folk Shadow Play	古代壁画 Ancient Chinese Mural Painting
中华传统美德 Chinese Traditional Virtues	中国古代帝王 Emperors of China	古代衡器 Ancient Weighing Apparatus
中国姓氏 Chinese Surnames	中国陶器 Chinese Pottery Ware	24节气 The Twenty-four Solar Terms
传统家具 Chinese Furniture	中国漆器 Chinese Lacquer Articles	中国名泉 Famous Springs in China
中国名山 Renowned Chinese Mountains	中国名寺 Famous Temples in China	长江黄河 Yangtze River and Yellow River
中国染织 Chinese Dyeing and Weaving	中国石窟 Grottoes in China	传统杂技 Traditional Acrobatic Arts
武术 Chinese Martial Arts	中国古桥 Ancient Bridges in China	中国婚俗 Marriage Customs in China
民间玩具 Folk Toys	中国古塔 Ancient Pagodas in China	匾额对联 Inscribed Tablets and Couplets
古代教育 Education in Ancient China	中国民居 Traditional Civil Residents	中国建筑装饰 Chinese Architectural Decoration
中国神话传说 Chinese Mythology and Legends	民间戏曲 Traditional Folk Operas	十二生肖 The Twelve Animals Represent Years
古代游戏 Recreational Games in Ancient China	中国灯彩 Colorful Chinese Lanterns and Lamps	佩饰 Ornaments Wore by Ancient Chinese
四大名著 Four Masterpieces of Chinese Fiction	诸子百家 Traditional Philosophers and Ideologists	文房清供 Stationery and Bibelot in Ancient Studies
古代科技 Ancient China's Science and Technology	中国牌坊 Chinese Decorated and Memorial Archways	中国祥禽瑞兽 Auspicious Beasts and Fowls in Chinese Culture
金银器 Gold and Silver Wares	中国茶艺 Chinese Tea Appreciation Ceremony	
竹木牙角器 Art Crafts Make of Bamboo, Wood, Ivory and Horn	秦砖汉瓦 Brick of Qin Dynasty and Tile of Han Dynasty	

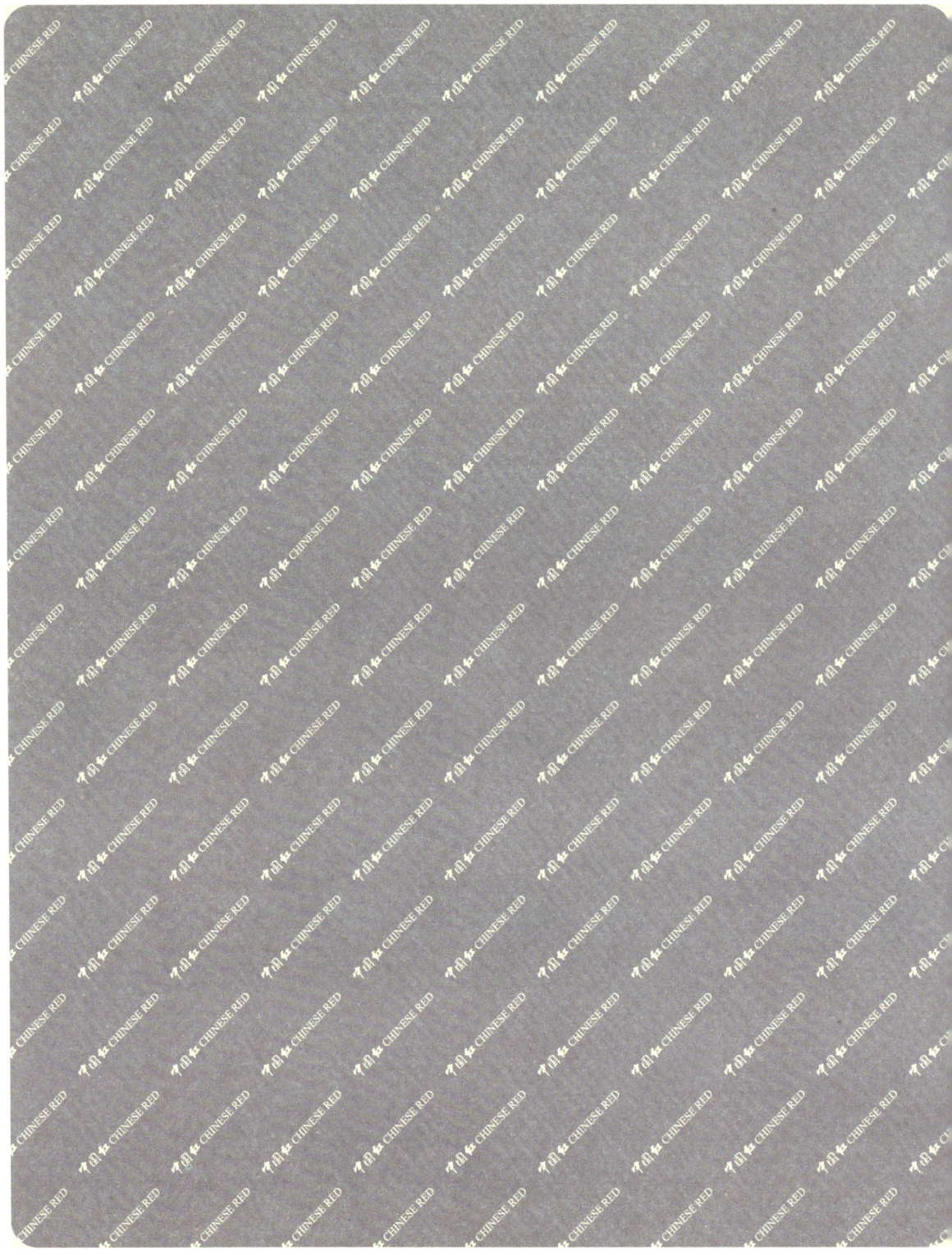